THE WRECK DIVING MANUAL

D1615625

The Wreck Diving Manual

Lizzie Bird

The Crowood Press

First published in 1997 by
The Crowood Press Ltd
Ramsbury, Marlborough
Wiltshire SN8 2HR

British Library Cataloguing-in-Publication Data
A catalogue record for this book is available from the British Library.

ISBN 1 86126 023 7

Picture Credits
Photographs by the author except for the following: AP Valves (page 96);
Aquascan International Ltd (page 29 bottom); Bob Brading (pages 2, 6, 7, 8, 9, 10
bottom, 15, 34, 44 top, 51 top, 58, 80, 81 top, 90 top, 90 bottom, 107, 108, 118
top, 139, 149, 150); Rod Davis (page 49); Ken Farrow (pages 57, 91 and 95 top);
Peter Mitchell, Sound Diving Publications (pages 32 bottom, 33, 51 bottom, 92
top and bottom, and 93 top and bottom); Mike Rowley (page 50 top); Mike Smith
(pages 11, 12, 13, 16, 23, 25, 29 top left and right, 29 bottom, 32, 35, 45, 48, 59,
61, 62, 63 left and right, 64, 65 top and bottom, 66 top and bottom, 67, 69 top
and bottom, 70, 71 top and bottom, 72 left, 76 left and right, 77 left and right, 81,
83, 95 bottom, 102 bottom, 103 top and bottom, 104, 105, 109, 110 left and
right, 111, 112, 113, 114, 115, 116, 118 bottom, 119 top and bottom, 120, 121
left and right, 123, 127, 130, 131, 134, 135, 136, 137, 138, 152, 153, 154, 155
and 156); and Uwatec (page 151).
The illustrations on pages 23, 29 (top left and right), 32 (top), 40 and 41 are reproduced by permission of the Controller of HMSO and the UK Hydrographic Office.
The illustration on page 11 is reproduced by permission of the Receiver of
Wreck, The Coastguard Agency.

Line drawings by the author.

Acknowledgements
To everyone who has helped in the preparation of this book but particularly
Mike Smith for all his support and photographs, and last but not least, Jack, my
long-suffering husband.

Throughout this book, 'he', 'him' and 'his' have been used as neutral pronouns
and refer to both males and females.

Typefaces used: text, Optima; headings, M Plantin.

Typeset and designed by
D & N Publishing
Membury Business Park, Lambourn Woodlands
Hungerford, Berkshire.

Printed and bound in Great Britain by WBC Book Manufacturers Limited,
Mid Glamorgan.

Contents

Introduction

Ask most people what they visualize when the word 'wreck' is mentioned and they will probably describe an old car: bent, battered and rusting with holes and with anything of value stripped off.

Say 'wreck' to a diver and they will immediately visualize an underwater dive site generally covering quite a large area. It will probably be a bent, battered and rusting structure with holes and with most items of value stripped off. However, a diver imagining the underwater wreck will also have a gleam in his eye, whether remembering a previous wreck dive or anticipating a new one. Why? What makes an underwater wreck so different from a land-based wreck? The word 'wreck' to a diver means 'ship wreck'.

Ships, either sailing or powered, no matter what size or type, always attract the attention of almost everyone who sees them on rivers, lakes or at sea. Perhaps it is the romanticism of a ship, perhaps the marvel of maritime engineering, perhaps the sheer size and the fact that it still floats! And this appreciation is when it is seen on the surface!

When a ship sinks it becomes an underwater stationery body that only a diver or submersible vehicle can reach, often too big to be moved and therefore subject to the ravages of time and the sea. The wreck, no matter what condition it went down in,

Marine life on a wreck.

Wreck shapes and light – a photographer's paradise.

loading and shifting cargoes, or design faults have resulted in sinkings. Ships have been drawn onto rocks by wreckers' lights or scuttled on purpose to claim insurance. And last, but by no means least, wars have caused a huge number of shipwrecks around the world.

Are divers interested in diving wrecks because of a morbid interest in the after-effects of a probable tragedy? The answer is 'no'. For divers a wreck is a tangible link with the world above the water surface, comforting as something that is recognizable but surrounded by the unknown. A wreck may be the nearest any diver will have come to a large ship. It is rare to have the freedom to explore from bow to stern when ships are in port or naval dockyards as there are always restrictions to access. Underwater, the ship has no barriers, no security guards, no 'tickets only' to board. The only restrictions to exploration are the divers' self-imposed ones of depth and time, the state of the wreck and water conditions on the wreck site. In some instances there are restrictions where a wreck has been designated a War Grave, Historical Wreck or is subject to other restrictive legislation by the relevant government.

This book will hopefully introduce wreck diving to divers at the beginning of their sports diving experience, broaden knowledge for those who are already diving wrecks and outline techniques that can be developed for more adventurous wreck diving. Some of the techniques don't apply only to diving wrecks but to a broad spectrum of dive sites a diver will visit.

will alter dramatically over a period of time. It will evolve to become part of the underwater domain, become colonized by the myriad of sea creatures who will claim it for their own. The ship, now a wreck, will continue its existence but as a man-made reef for many years.

Ships rarely go down through choice, but a number of vessels have been purposely sunk around the world to provide underwater reefs to encourage marine life colonization and promote the diving tourist industry. Otherwise, ships sink for a number of reasons. Navigation errors have caused ships to sink when they have struck reefs, rocks, or coastlines. Sinking may have been caused by hitting another ship or floating object such as an iceberg. Factors affecting a ship's stability, such as bad weather, high seas, poor

1 Wrecks

In an ideal underwater world, the wreck will be sitting upright on the seabed, complete as it was on the surface. There are some wrecks like this but they are rare.

Generally, when a ship sinks, the damage it has sustained on the surface, the water pressure on the way down and tidal currents all combine to crush and break up her structure. At the same time, water rushes in, flooding some compartments, though maybe missing others. Quite quickly the ship is surrounded by forces it was not designed to withstand and as it sinks deeper, the pressures increase. The ship may twist and turn as air pockets try to rise to the surface but are trapped by the structure. Some of the ship's superstructure, those parts above the main deck, may be torn and swept away and the main structure, the hull, may collapse or be split apart. By the time the ship hits the seabed it may already be in sections. The impact on the seabed will cause further damage and scatter parts over a wide area. The pieces that have been swept away on the way down will themselves sink and leave a trail of debris on the seabed leading to the place where the main body of the wreck eventually comes to rest.

If a ship is stranded on rocks or the shoreline, wave action will grind and pound the vessel as it is held fast. The force of the waves may break it apart into large sections and then each section may be broken into further pieces. Wreck debris will be scattered and carried to and fro and may be deposited some considerable distance from the original wreck site.

The sinking ship, twisting and turning, leaves a debris trail to where it eventually lies on the seabed.

The wreck of the Inverlane, *Scapa Flow, the Orkneys.*

Photographic opportunities.

The Attraction of Diving Wrecks

The sinking of a ship is in many cases a violent act, and the sea lays claim to these man-made chunks of metal or wood. The eroding process begins almost immediately. Water, sand and stones will scour the wreck and this action may increase in storm conditions. The natural decay of the ship's fabric begins with metal rusting and wood rotting. What were once ship's holds become caverns, and living quarters become transformed into small caves. Broken masts, spars and plate create overhangs and crevices. Marine life starts to colonize and integrate the wreck into its environment and ecosystem.

For the underwater photographer the marine life, structure, shapes and light filtering down from the surface offer a wealth of opportunities. For the diver interested in marine biology, the wreck can offer a large diversity of life that uses the wreck site for shelter or a hunting ground. For the diver hunter-gatherer, this man-made reef becomes a big larder. (Note: It is not advisable to have the diver photographer and the diver hunter-gatherer dive together on a wreck!)

The diver explorer takes delight in being the one to discover and

Cross-section of a wreck showing 'caves' and overhangs.

identify parts of a wreck. A wreck, from the moment it sinks, becomes a time capsule. Items from the ship and its cargo, or anything used on the ship, may be found from the ship's bell to pieces of china used in the galley, from portholes to bags of cement (solidified!) or even tractors.

What are the ownership implications when discovering or recovering anything from a wreck? The Coastguard Agency's Receiver of Wreck has kindly supplied the following information:

The Receiver of Wreck, located within the Coastguard Agency, is responsible for the administration of the Merchant Shipping Acts 1995 dealing with wreck and salvage and operates on behalf of the Department of Transport.

The definition of the word 'wreck' is flotsam, jetsam, derelict and lagan found in or on the shores of the sea or any tidal water. It includes a ship, aircraft, or hovercraft,

parts of these, their cargo or equipment. It may be of antique or archaeological value such as gold coins, or a yacht or dinghy abandoned at sea, or items such a drums of chemicals or crates of foodstuffs. **Flotsam** *means goods lost from a ship which has sunk or otherwise*

Leaflet obtainable from the Coastguard about what to do if you turn up something.

Collection of bottles from wreck dives and clay pipe found in sand beside a wreck. The pipe is leaning against a cannonball.

perished, which are recoverable by reason of their remaining afloat.

Jetsam means goods cast overboard in order to lighten a vessel which is in danger of being sunk, not withstanding that afterwards it perishes.

Derelict means property, whether vessel or cargo, which has been abandoned and deserted at sea by those who were in charge of it without any hope of recovering it.

Lagan means goods cast overboard from a ship which afterwards perishes, these goods buoyed so as to render them recoverable.

It is a legal requirement that all recovered wreck is reported to the Receiver of Wreck, whether recovered from within or outside of UK territorial waters and even if the finder is the owner. If a wreck is found then contact should be made with the Receiver of Wreck or local Coastguard station. The reason to report wreck is to give the legitimate owner the opportunity of recovering their property.

The Receiver of Wreck will investigate ownership of the wreck items. The owner has one year in which to come forward and prove title to the property. During this statutory period, the finder may be allowed to hold the wreck on behalf of the Receiver of Wreck, whilst the investigations are carried out.

Wreck recovered from within UK waters which remains unclaimed at the end of the one year statutory period becomes the property of the Crown and the Receiver of Wreck is required to dispose of it. Disposal may be through sale or auction, although in many instances the finder will be allowed to keep items of unclaimed wreck in lieu of a salvage award. This, however, is at the discretion of the Receiver of Wreck and each case is judged on its merits.

Historical wrecks For the purposes of the Merchant Shipping Act, historic wreck is defined as items which are over 100 years old. The Coastguard Agency is committed to try, wherever practical, to offer items of historic wreck to institutions where they will remain accessible to the public and such items are offered first to Registered Museums. Wherever practical the Receiver of Wreck will endeavour to ensure that the artifacts are offered to a museum within the area of the find site and will consider the finder's wishes with regard to this whenever possible. The Receiver of Wreck will liaise with the Department of National Heritage and other relevant organizations as necessary when dealing with historic wreck.

Historical wreck may have been discovered and registered as a Historical Wreck Site. This means the wreck is being archaeologically surveyed and possibly raised and is left to the experts to identify and perhaps recover the ship or artifacts. These sites are out of bounds to recreational divers unless they are officially involved in the registration and survey. Some sites do allow diving with a 'look, don't touch' policy. Historic Wreck Sites are marked on charts. In some cases there are notices on the shoreline in the vicinity of the wreck site while other sites are marked by a large yellow buoy with 'Historic Wreck' marked on it.

Navy vessels Generally a naval wreck has been caused by war

Mementos of wreck dives including a piece of coal!

action and involved loss of life. The Navy may have sealed the wreck as a War Grave and as such divers must respect and honour the site. It should remain as it is, undisturbed and peaceful, its presence a memorial to lives given and lost in the service of their country. In many cases no diving is allowed in the vicinity of a War Grave wreck; where diving is allowed it is only to look, not to remove anything. To take anything from a War Grave is desecration.

Dangerous wrecks Some wrecks are designated as dangerous wrecks and are not to be dived. These could be where the cargo being carried was dangerous, such as explosives, chemicals and so on. Most of these wrecks are cleared by the Navy but some do still exist. It could also be that the structure of the wreck is too fragile and deemed to be in danger of collapse.

So what about the small articles that you may find: the piece of cutlery, broken crockery, small pieces of brass from where a wreck has disintegrated? **All** recovery should be reported to the Receiver, together with a short description of where it was found and/or a photograph. In the majority of cases the Receiver will decide no further action is necessary and you will be allowed to retain those pieces as mementos of your dive.

This might sound very pernickety but it is possible that a broken piece of china with part of a crest or insignia may help to identify a wreck. If other divers have found the same and reported them perhaps your piece will link with theirs, rather like completing a jigsaw. The china may be from a known wreck but may indicate another wreck in the vicinity that is, as yet, unknown or older than first thought. However insignificant you think your 'find' is, remember that the Receiver has a much broader knowledge base than you do and a series of reported finds from one particular area builds into a larger pattern to indicate just what is down there on the seabed. Recreational divers have found and reported small, seemingly insignificant items that appeared to be quite old and subsequent archaeological surveys and excavations have revealed a historical wreck site.

The other important reason for reporting wreck recovery is that it belongs to somebody and by law should be reported. The Receiver has a responsibility to the owner of the wreck **as well as to you as the finder of wreck**. There may well be a salvage reward and the finder's rights are protected and taken care of by the Receiver.

Should you find something that you think poses a possible danger contact the Coastguard and they will investigate and make your find safe. Chemicals on the seabed that could have contaminated the marine environment and relics of wars that could have exploded have been found by divers.

Recreational divers have the opportunity to explore and see sights that relatively few others ever will. At the same time they have a duty to respect the marine environment, protect it for future generations and, by reporting and not hoarding their discoveries, play an important part in increasing the knowledge and appreciation of our maritime heritage.

2 Locating Wrecks

It sounds quite simple to state that where there is water, whether it be the sea, a river or a lake, there is likely to be a wreck of some description. In all probability this is true but the number of wrecks that recreational divers can dive are immediately restricted because:

• we have to know where they are to dive them
• we have to know whether it is permissible to dive them
• they have to be within our depth limitations as recreational divers
• water movement prevents diving at certain times.

So how do we find out about wrecks we can dive? There are a number of sources we can use.

Local Knowledge

Whether a wreck disaster has involved a local community, or a fishing boat has caught nets or lines on something underwater, someone local will know where, and probably quite a lot else about that particular site. The wreck knowledge permeates through the community and fishermen, dive centres or shops and local divers will know the site. A salvage company may well have worked on the wreck and taken anything of value, but left behind a good wreck dive.

Local knowledge also helps to provide up-to-date information on the state of the wreck. Has it collapsed since discovery owing to storms? Has it recently been heavily fished and are there likely to be lines or nets on the wreck? Have parts of the wreck, once identifiable, now disappeared?

Dive Guides

Based on local knowledge and extensive research, dive guides have been produced to give the diver a more complete picture of the type of wreck. The British Sub-Aqua Club produces Wreck Registers that also give details of many diveable wrecks around the British Isles.

Where a wreck has been identified the research work might include photographs of what the ship looked like, a plan of the ship, what it was carrying and a drawing of what it now looks like on the seabed. The guides advise on depth and the best state of the tide to dive the wreck. Some also include information on marine life to be found there. Where the wreck is unidentified the historical information may be more sketchy.

The guides might also include wrecks that have not as yet been found. The last known position or

Dive guides.

sighting may be given but previous dives on the site have not located anything. If a diver is then lucky enough to find wreckage in the vicinity, could it be one of these wrecks? A piece of wreckage might yield the identity of the ship and the guide gives an idea of the possible options.

Further Research

It may be that more information is wanted on an identified wreck, or that divers want to do their own research on an unidentified wreck. It could also be your great luck to discover an unknown wreck and want to establish what it is, whether it is really unknown or whether someone has already found it. Remember, whether a wreck is known or unknown, someone will have claim to it, so consider whether it can it be dived at all. This is when research is needed by

turning to various bodies with listings of shipwrecks. Chapter 12 outlines research procedures to assist the wreck researcher.

With so much information to hand about a wreck, how can it be located? It would be very useful to have a floating signpost to mark the wreck site. There are indeed some marine signposts where a wreck is deemed to be a hazard to navigation at sea; it could be marked by a special buoy.

The position of a wreck can be given in a number of ways, a charted position in latitude and longitude, a set of transits, or transits

with compass bearings. A combination of both charted position and transits increase the likelihood of finding the site. Without electronic navigation systems using latitude and longitude readouts, divers depend upon transits, compass bearings and use of echo sounders to 'read' the configuration of the seabed, with varying success. However, carefully chosen transits may offer the greatest accuracy for relocating a wreck site.

Charted Wreck Position

Wreck positions are usually given using latitude and longitude. There is no need to panic, however, and turn to the end of this chapter! If you cannot get your brain around 'lats. and longs.' perhaps the following explanation will help.

Charts are maps of the sea; in marine terminology the word 'chart' is always used. Road maps are a coded representation of how the land would look with its features of towns and roads drawn to a scale. Charts are the same but concentrate on the sea and particular features, mainly danger areas, to navigate ships safely. Of the many danger marks, one is of particular interest to divers: wrecks!

The scale of a chart can either be large (great detail, small area) or small (simpler detail but greater area). In other words, a large-scale chart will give a great deal of information on a relatively small area, such as a harbour entrance, and a small-scale chart covers a large area with less detailed information giving a general overview of an expanse of coastline and sea. What is going to be of interest to wreck divers is mostly shown on the larger scale charts where dangers are marked for

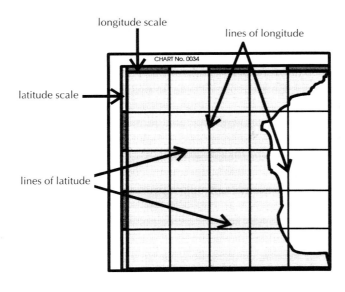

Lines of latitude and longitude on a chart.

shipping with greater accuracy and these include rocks, reefs and, of course, wrecks in coastal waters.

Chart makers face the problem of representing on a flat piece of paper the seas of the world. The world is a sphere (for purists it is oblate flattened at the poles) and transferring a round shape to a flat surface will always mean distortion. However, chart makers have allowed for this by drawing charts as 'projections' using mathematical formulae – Mercator projection and Gnomic projection are the most common.

If planning to sail single handed around the world, the chart projection used is important but, fortunately for divers, the charts we use cover very small areas so we don't have to worry about projection allowances.

Just as a road map uses a grid reference system, so does a chart. Look at a chart and you will see that along each side are numbered scales. The scale at the bottom and top of the chart measures longitude. The scale at the sides of the chart measures latitude. Lines of latitude and longitude drawn on a chart produce a lattice or grid.

Two base points are needed from which to lay out this world grid.

Longitude

Imagine the world with the north and south poles clearly marked. Cutting through the world from pole to pole would result in two half globes. The circumference or outer edge of a half globe is a circle known as a great circle when referred to in charts and navigation. If we put the globe back together any circle drawn around the globe that passes through both poles would be a great circle. Therefore, as they always measure the same circumference, they can be used as a base for measurements. These great circles, called meridians, are also known as lines of longitude (lying longways).

For a grid reference there has to be a starting point. By international agreement the meridian (line of

Lines of longitude.

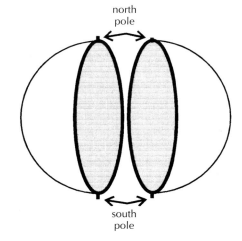

north pole

south pole

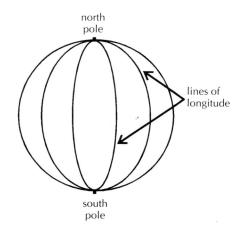

north pole

lines of longitude

south pole

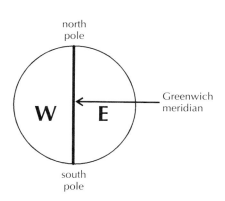

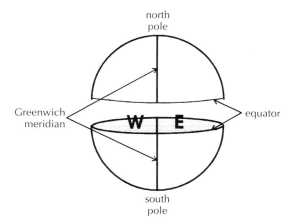

longitude) that passes through Greenwich in Britain is known as 'the prime meridian'. The prime or Greenwich meridian divides the world into two half globes: one half to the west and one half to the east. But we need further meridians for the grid reference system and to know which half of the world is being referred to.

If the world is cut in half again, but this time through the equator and at right angles to the prime meridian we end up with two half circles of 180° degrees to west and east. If lines are drawn from the centre of the earth to the edge of the half circles, their angle can be measured using the Greenwich meridian as a base line of 0°. This gives their position relative to the Greenwich meridian so lines of longitude will read up to 180° to the west or to the east.

The Greenwich meridian divides the world into west and east.

180° to east and west.

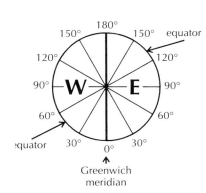

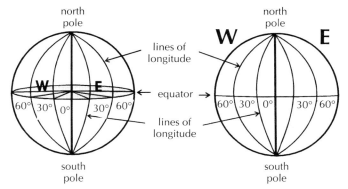

Latitude

To complete a grid system we need horizontal lines, lines that lie sideways. For the world grid system these are called the lines or parallels of latitude, and they are also measured using the equator plane and the centre of the earth. Imagine the inside of the world scooped out except for the equator plane and a rod joining the poles. This rod passes through the centre of the equator plane and, therefore, the centre of the earth. The angle measured at the centre of the earth to one or other of the poles will be no more than 90° to the equator plane. Imagine a pencil held at a 50° angle from the equator plane at the centre of the earth If you rotated the pencil around this centre point, not changing the angle, the pencil line would mark a circle on the earth's surface parallel to the equator circle and always at 50°;

Scooped-out world (left); line of latitude (right).

this is a parallel of latitude. Using the equator for reference, we can identify the parallels of latitude as being above or below it; in other words to the **North** or **South**.

The lines of latitude and longitude are the earth's grid and can be used to locate a particular position on the earth's surface in either north, south, east or west quadrants. However, we need to have measurements to add to this base information.

Subdivisions

The measurement of the circumference of the equator is used as the base for our world grid. If we drew lines at 1° intervals out from the centre of the world on the equator plane, the 360 lines would fan out like the spokes of a wheel. Where the lines meets the circumference of the equator a measurement can be made between each degree – it will

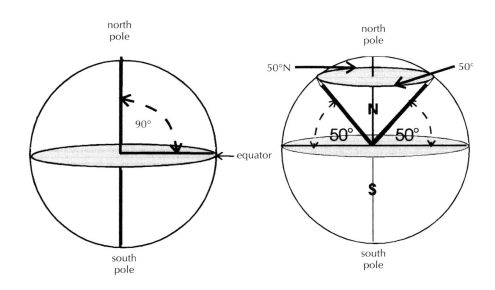

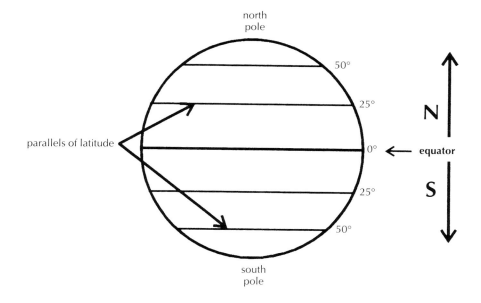

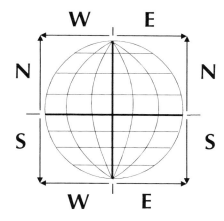

The earth's quadrants.

mariners it was given the name 'nautical mile' abbreviated to nm.

The circumference of the equator =
1° = 60nm × 360 = 21,600nm

So 1° = 60' = 60 nautical miles. This is quite a distance, so for accuracy of measurement it needs further subdivision. The obvious subdivision is to use seconds which were used in the past but now, for even greater accuracy, we subdivide the minute into one hundredths.

We write the measurements as follows:

Parallels of latitude north and south of the equator.

always be the same. A degree is subdivided into minutes and the measurement of one minute on the equator is 6,080ft. Because this was more than the statute mile of 5,280ft it needed to be called something and as it was referring to charts and

50 degrees, 10 minutes, 60 hundredths as: 50°10'.60
30 degrees, 40 minutes, 20 hundredths as: 30°40'.20

Charts are flat, and representing the curved surface of the earth on

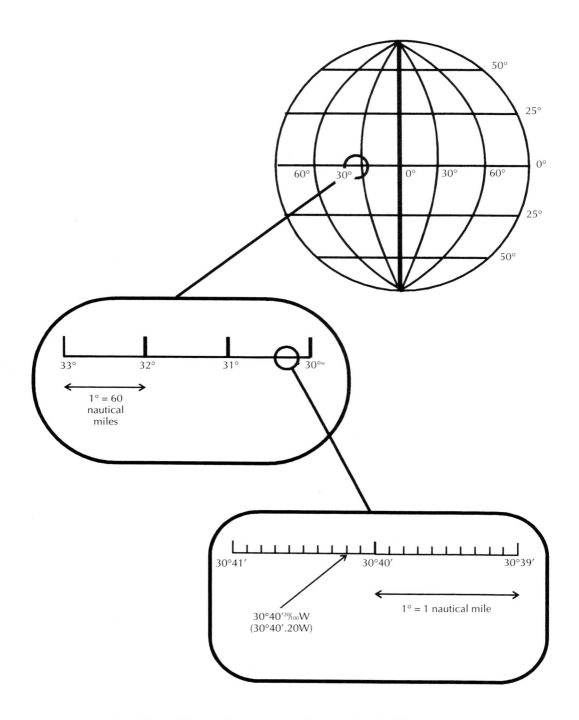

Subdivision of degrees (°) into minutes (') and one hundredths of a minute.

flat paper means there is distortion when meridian lines are straightened and latitude lines are stretched. However, this distortion is taken into account by chart makers using mathematical calculations, called projections. Most navigation charts used by divers use the principle that as one minute of latitude is equal to one minute of longitude at the equator, a scale can be calculated above and below the equator using the latitude scale for measurement. Remember, the latitude scale is read on the side of the chart. You should always use the latitude scale nearest to the area you are planning to work in to calculate distance measurements accurately.

Chart references always give latitude first and then longitude, and state whether the position is north or south of the equator and east or west of the Greenwich meridian. The previous example would need the following additions to mark the exact position:

50°10'.60 N
30°40'.20 W

Using this grid reference we can mark one precise position on the world. If we omitted the N and W, our grid reference could place us north or south of the equator and east or west of Greenwich!

Finding the Wreck at Sea

A known wreck position can be marked on a chart using latitude and longitude measurements but,

unfortunately, these lines are not marked on the sea surface!

Prior to electronic navigation systems, the guiding of vessels by using the stars (celestial navigation), or by sight along coastlines (pilotage) took years of experience and study. Electronic navigation systems, once expensive, are now within the reach of most sea users and a basic understanding of navigation is all that is required to use them. Although easy to use, they do not necessarily make people better seafarers; that still takes practice and time.

Use the side of the chart, the latitude scale, for distance measurement.

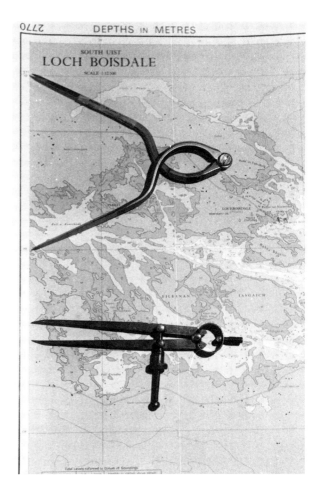

The importance of adding N or S, E or W to mark correct position.

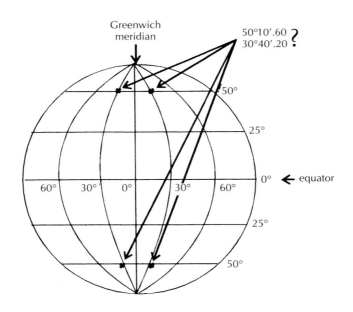

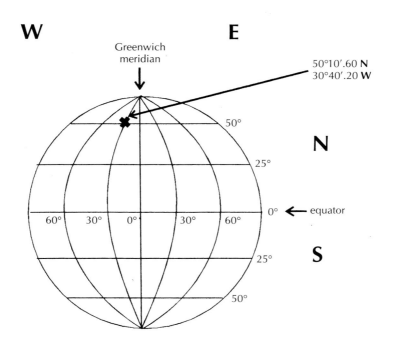

Electronic navigation systems locate their position on the globe by receiving signals from transmitting stations that are set at specific positions. The transmitters send electronic signals to a boat's receiver unit, which works out its distance from each transmitter from the time the signal takes to get to the boat. The distance from each transmitter is then combined to give an exact position on the earth's surface. This position is displayed in the form of latitude and longitude measurements and can be noted and used to plot the receiver's and, therefore, the boat's position on a chart.

Two systems currently in use around UK coastal waters are Decca and GPS. Decca works on radio signals issued by ground stations and GPS, or Global Positioning System, works using radio signals sent from satellites which are constantly circling the earth. The satellites move around the earth on preset orbits and are set up to know exactly where they are in relation to the earth at all times during their orbits. A position is fixed using information from at least three satellites.

GPS receiving units have dramatically decreased in price over recent years and can be bought as fixed units for larger boats or as hand-held receivers, ideal for smaller boats. The receiver unit, as well as identifying where it is, thus giving the boat's position, can also give information about how to get to the wreck's given position. If a wreck's position is entered in latitude and longitude into the receiver's memory, the system will work out the distance from the boat to the wreck's position. It will calculate how to get there, that is, what direction to steer, and constantly update progress towards that site.

Once wreck site information has been entered into electronic navigation systems it can be stored in the memory and recalled for future use. There may be slight anomalies in both the Decca and GPS systems so that they will not take you back to the exact same spot every time, but in general they will always return you very near to the wreck site. If you can use other position fixing methods discussed below to add to the electronic position of the wreck so much the better.

Any navigation equipment needs practice to understand its capabilities. Manufacturers have detailed information and some offer small 'acquaint' courses with their products.

A hand-held GPS receiver; ideal for small boats.

Transit Position of Wrecks

Many wrecks lie around our coast. They sank in sight of land on their way to or from port or while trying to seek safe havens close to shore. Navigation errors in bad weather caused many wrecks along the coastline. If they did sink or founder within sight of land then there is a possibility of using the land and features that can be seen from the sea to locate the wreck site: these are called transits.

Transit lines are visual lines of sight lining up two features, thus putting you on a 'position line'. The greater the distance on land between the two objects used the better, especially if the distance between these two objects is greater than the distance between the nearest object and the eye.

More than one transit is needed, so that the position lines intersect and pinpoint the site of the wreck. Ideally these two transit position lines should be at a 90° angle from the viewer as wider or lesser angles reduce accuracy.

It's even better to find a third transit to use as this increases the accuracy even more. The way to use three transits is to 'Y' them. Approach from the sea along the central transit's position line and watch as the other two transits come into line. This is known as being 'on' the transit, the position fix of the wreck site.

The compass can be used to assist in relocating transits by looking in the right direction. A compass can also be useful at times when only one transit is available, so a compass bearing of another single feature is necessary. Keeping the boat on the bearing in the direction of the feature and lining up onto the

A single transit.

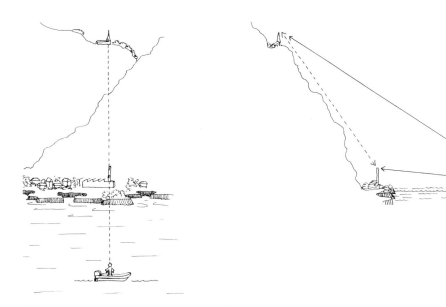

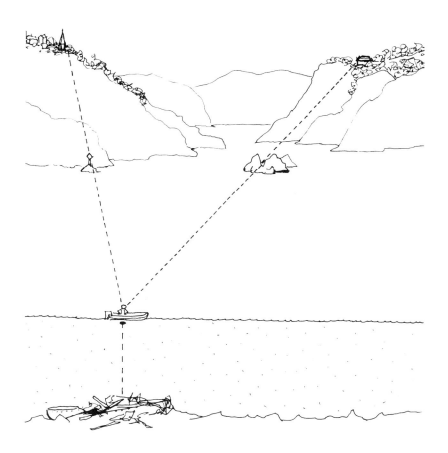

Two transits.

transit can work, but maintaining a steady course is quite difficult and the margin of error increases. The wreck needs to be quite large or spread over a wide area for this method to be successful.

Compass bearings of land features located on their own or with an instrument called a sextant can be used from a boat should you locate a site of interest by accident and successfully mark it with a shot line or a diver's surface marker buoy (*see* later chapters). It will be almost impossible to relocate using the compass or the sextant from a boat affected by

sea movement, but you can transfer the information collected and identify the position on a chart. This information can then be transferred to an electronic navigation system to use as a fix to start a future search.

Below the Surface

So far, we have been locating wreck positions using surface information but we also need to know what is beneath us. A chart will give information about the nature of the seabed surrounding the wreck.

27

Three transits and the 'Y' position.

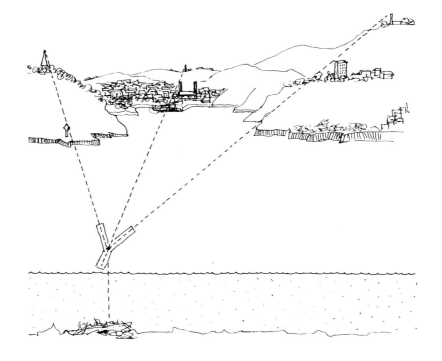

Admiralty Hydrographic publication 5011; the key to all chart symbols.

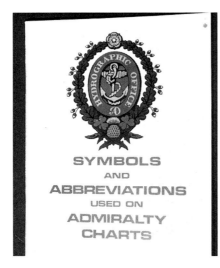

Interpreting the signs and abbreviations that are found on charts can be achieved with Admiralty Hydrographic publication 5011. Included in this are descriptions of the seabed: rock, sand, shale, mud, and so on. 5011 is also very useful for identifying coastline features that may be used for transits.

Having found our surface wreck position it would be good to see below the sea surface and check the accuracy of our position. Another piece of equipment ideal for divers' use is a depth sounder, also called an echo sounder. Not only does the sounder give us the depth to the seabed but the display indicates the shape and nature of the seabed. It works by sending out ultrasonic sound waves from a transducer fixed to the hull of the boat. The sound waves echo back from the seabed and are received by the transducer. The length of time it takes for the 'echo' to be transmitted and received back is measured by the equipment and computed to the screen to read as a visual depth display of what is below the transducer.

If a wreck stands clear of sand, the display will show very clearly the rise and fall of the wreck shape. Unfortunately, this is not always the case. Ships hit rocks and rocks can also look like wrecks to an echo sounder! With practice and diving the site a number of times, the particular shape of the wreck as it shows on the screen may become recognizable. Colour visual display units have enhanced the recognizable features even more than the original black and white screens.

There have been numerous programmes on TV showing serious wreck hunters using equipment called Side Scan Sonar. This instrument scans sideways along the seabed still working on the 'echo' principle and will give a clear representation of any wreck found. Unfortunately, these sets are quite

An echo sounder which can easily be fitted into a small boat.

29

Principle of an echo sounder.

expensive but, as with all technology, their price is slowly decreasing as smaller units are being made.

Some manufacturers now incorporate echo-sounding equipment into their electronic navigation units. The unit can position fix and echo sound at the same time producing a side-by-side visual display.

Another method of detecting a wreck is to use a proton magnetometer. The earth acts like a large magnet with magnetic lines of force connecting the two poles much the same as a simple bar magnet. The lines of force can be distorted by placing another metal object nearby. A wreck, in most cases, is a large ferrous object and this creates a local variation or anomaly, and slightly alters the earth's magnetic field at that site. A proton magnet-

ometer can detect these anomalies. It consists of a sensing unit, known as 'the fish', which is towed underwater behind a boat and is linked by a cable to a control unit in the boat. The control unit is set to a 'no anomaly' mode with a +/- dial and utilizes a visual display screen or audible regular pulse.

As the fish is towed behind the boat it 'reads' the magnetic force lines of the earth and, passing over or near ferrous material, detects the local anomaly and relays the information to the control unit. This sets off an audible and visual alarm, allowing a small shot marker to be placed in the water; a second shot should be deployed as the anomaly subsides. Several passes over the area from four points of the compass will result in a pattern of shots,

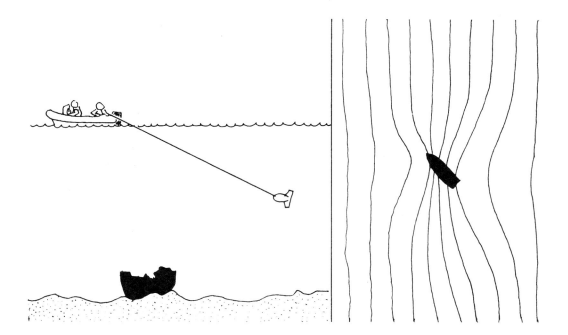

surrounding the ferrous 'lump' on the seabed.

Learning how to understand the information received by the unit does take practice and patience as well as an understanding of search techniques using this equipment. Some manufacturers and suppliers offer short training courses. If you plan to wreck hunt with this system, ensure that somebody on board knows how to use and interpret the information.

It is very tempting to rely totally on electronic aids to find wrecks, but lift your eyes away from the screens and look for other clues. The surface of the sea can look different where there is an underwater rock as the water moves around and over it. A wreck can also cause different sea surface patterns. There may well be other divers who have marked the wreck with a buoy to come back to at a later date. It has been known for divers to spend a long time glued to their VDUs when a quick glance up would have alerted them to the presence of a large buoy in the near vicinity and divers do not mark uninteresting things for future dives!

Another point should be borne in mind when using electronic aids; they are just that, aids. They should not replace basic navigation skills and seamanship when out at sea. They can break down or run out of battery power just when they are needed most!

The proton magneto-meter's 'fish' towed behind a boat (left) will detect the local anomaly to the earth's magnetic force lines (right) caused by the wreck.

3 Dive Planning for Wreck Dives

The most important consideration in planning a wreck dive is the depth and type of wreck. A deep, dark wreck is hardly suitable for introducing wreck diving to inexperienced divers. A shallow, light wreck with lots of life may sound ideal but, if it is covered in fishing nets, the dive could become a nightmare.

Diver on a shallow wreck site.

Which Wreck to Dive?

A little preliminary research through local knowledge and wreck guides will outline the type of wreck dive to expect.

Most shallow wrecks, in a range of up to 20m depth, have been torn

apart and spread out by wave action. Some of these are ideal wrecks to dive as a 'first wreck dive'. Marine life is usually very active in shallower waters and, although at first appearance a wreck can appear as a pile of twisted, rusting metal, some features can usually be found that identify that it was once a ship. The disadvantage of quite a few shallow wrecks is that, being fairly close to the shoreline, the underwater visibility may be reduced. This can be caused by the nature of the seabed, river outfalls nearby carrying land sediment into the sea or wave action constantly stirring the surrounding site. Those wrecks in sheltered coastal waters, where water movement is reduced, often silt over and, as soon as fin touches metal, a cloud of silty particles rise to obscure what before looked very interesting.

However, it's not all bad news for shallow wrecks. Some lie in or near tidal waters and are swept by water action, clearing away silt and carrying food particles for marine life. Light filters down from the surface and diving can be as good as at any coral reef in exotic climes. The wealth of life and colour can be quite spectacular even though the water temperature is a little cooler! Some shallow wrecks can make excellent night dives in calm weather, with good underwater visibility and with little or no current.

Diver on a deeper wreck where larger chunks of wreckage may be found.

Wrecks in the depth range of 20–30m generally offer slightly more 'ship shapes' to identify. Depending on how they sank, some even look like ships with the hull clearly identifiable. Those that have suffered huge damage on the surface prior to sinking may be scattered over a sizeable area but perhaps in larger chunks than the shallower wrecks. Again sea life is usually prolific, and bright surface light and good visibility can make these wrecks excellent dives.

Below 30m and to the recreational divers' maximum depth of 50m lie the deeper wrecks. Larger pieces of wreckage can be found, undisturbed by wave action or even, perhaps, the complete ship only damaged by the reason for sinking.

Some of the deeper wrecks appear almost complete but worn by the erosion of the marine environment. Although generally darker, as light is absorbed by suspended particles in the water, the marine life can be good as the wreck offers protection to the deeper sea fish life. A prominent wreck on a flat seabed can be easy to find using an echo sounder and as an artificial reef that attracts larger fish, these may be seen on the sounder before the wreck shows. Quite a few of these deeper wreck sites have been located by fishing boats discovering excellent fishing grounds. If so, then always be aware that where there is fishing there are nets and lines, and hooks!

You never quite know what you may find. A dive on the same wreck, in different tidal conditions, at a different time of year will become a totally new experience.

Pre-Planning the Wreck Dive

Pre-planning any dive before arriving on the dive site is good diving practice. Possible problems should be considered well in advance of the actual dive as this ensures that divers will dive in the safest and most enjoyable conditions and have the correct equipment available for the particular dive planned (and packed for!).

Depth

As for all dive planning, we must know our maximum depth for the

A deep wreck, almost complete.

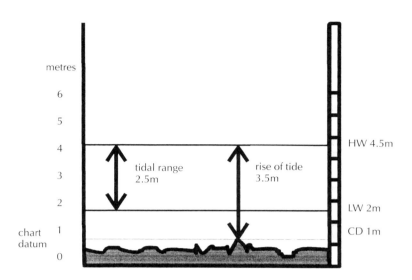

Chart datum.

dive. From this we can calculate, using tables or computers, the dive time, decompression regime and air requirements.

The depth of a wreck can be ascertained from the chart. The depth shown is known as chart datum. This is calculated by hydrographers to be the lowest water level predictable using detailed astronomical factors. Charted depths do not include the actual depth of water

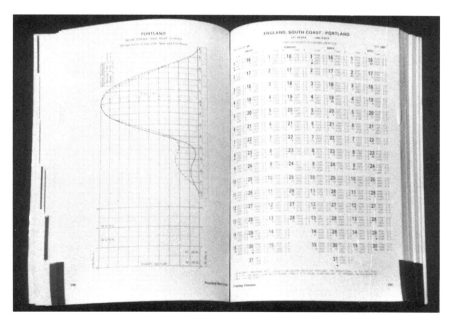

A set of tide tables gives information about what depth can be expected on the wreck site.

above that charted figure. To find out what the range of water depth is, remembering that the tide floods and ebbs, in other words goes in and out, we need to find out some more information. A set of tide tables will be needed for the region in which the wreck lies. Dive shops, chandlers and fishing tackle shops normally stock local tables. Nautical almanacs and the Hydrographic Office produce tide tables for all UK waters.

If you watched the sea over a period of a week or so, you would notice that the level of high water or low water varies from day to day. From very high to very low, or less high and less low. If you looked at a set of tide tables for that period you would see that the tidal range, the difference between high water and low water, changes; spring tides cover the greater range and neaps the lesser range. Spring tides occur on or up to two days after the new moon and the full moon, and a neap tide occurs half way between the new and full moon. It isn't just the moon that affects the tides, but a combination of the sun, the earth and the moon's gravitational forces; tides are greatest when all three are

in line (termed 'syzygy'), and smaller when the moon moves in its orbit around the earth away from this 'gravitational' line (quadrature).

In some tide tables moon symbols indicating spring tides can be seen on particular dates:

o   new moon
●   full moon

To find out the expected depth on a dive the HW (high water) and LW (low water) times are given in the tide tables for every day of the year. If, for example, the charted depth for a wreck is given as 20m, this is the highest point of the wreck, look up the tide information for the day the wreck dive is planned. For example, if the table says:

LW   05.30 1.5m
HW   11.30 4.5m

This means that low water (LW) is at 05.30 and at that time there will be 1.5m of water above chart datum. On the wreck at 20m chart datum the actual depth will 21.5m at low water. Six hours later at 11.30 is high water (HW), and the table tells you that there will be 4.5m of water

Syzygy
spring tides – sun, moon and earth in line

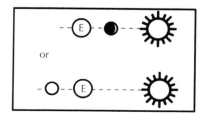

Quadrature
neap tides – moon not in line with sun or earth

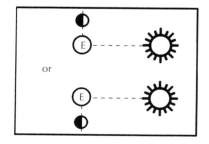

Spring and neap tides.

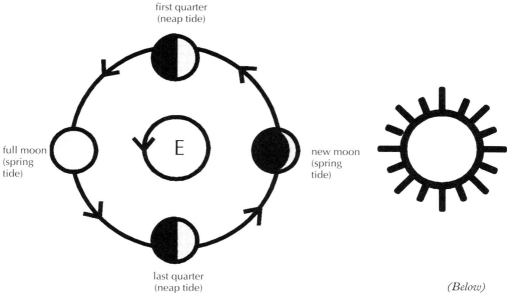

first quarter
(neap tide)

full moon
(spring
tide)

E

new moon
(spring
tide)

last quarter
(neap tide)

the moon orbits the earth about once a month

the earth rotates around its axis about once a day

(Below)
Example of the
differences in
HW and LW
on spring and
neap tides.

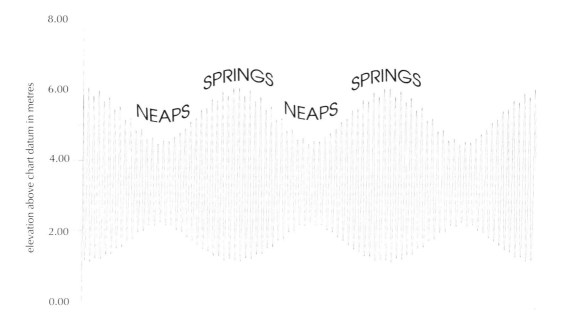

8.00

6.00

elevation above chart datum in metres

4.00

2.00

0.00

SPRINGS

NEAPS

SPRINGS

NEAPS

The tidal range.

charted wreck depth	20.0m			20.0m
05.30 low water	1.5m	11.30 high water		4.5m
actual depth LW	21.5m	actual depth HW		24.5m
tidal range				3m

above chart datum. The actual depth above the wreck will be 24.5m wreck depth chart datum 20m + 4.5m. Between 05.30 and 11.30 the depth will increase from 21.5m to 24.5m, a total of 3m, and this is what is called the 'tidal range'. A simple table can help (*see* above).

Working out the Depth of Water

To find out the expected depth between 05.30 and 11.30 at a particular time two methods can be used.

One method is called the 'rule of twelfths'. Find out the tidal range, in

---

Rule of Twelfths

Charted depth of wreck = 20m

$$
\begin{aligned}
\text{Height at LW} &= 21.5\text{m}\\
\text{Height at HW} &= 24.5\text{m}\\
\text{Tidal range} &= 3\text{m}\\
\tfrac{1}{12} &= 0.25\text{m}
\end{aligned}
$$

Time	0530–0630	0630–0730	0730–0830	0830–0930	0930–1030	1030–1130
	$\frac{1}{12}$	$\frac{2}{12}$	$\frac{3}{12}$	$\frac{3}{12}$	$\frac{2}{12}$	$\frac{1}{12}$
						0.25m
					0.25m	0.25m
					0.25m	0.25m
				0.25m	0.25m	0.25m
				0.25m	0.25m	0.25m
				0.25m	0.25m	0.25m
			0.25m	0.25m	0.25m	0.25m
			0.25m	0.25m	0.25m	0.25m
			0.25m	0.25m	0.25m	0.25m
		0.25m	0.25m	0.25m	0.25m	0.25m
		0.25m	0.25m	0.25m	0.25m	0.25m
	0.25m	0.25m	0.25m	0.25m	0.25m	0.25m
	+	+	+	+	+	+
LW height	21.5m	21.5m	21.5m	21.5m	21.5m	21.5m
actual depth	21.75m	22.25m	23.0m	23.75m	24.25m	24.5m

---

this case 3m, and divide by 12. This gives a figure of one twelfth, 0.25m.

In the first hour, the tide rises by one twelfth
In the second hour, the tide rises by two more twelfths
In the third hour, the tide rises by three more twelfths
In the fourth hour, the tide rises by three more twelfths
In the fifth hour, the tide rises by two more twelfths
In the sixth hour, the tide rises by one more twelfth
Again, a table can help work this out.

Whenever using tide tables you need to remember that in the UK clocks are put forward one hour in the summer – British Summer Time (BST). Tide tables are timed at Greenwich Mean Time (GMT). So for BST you need to add an hour onto the table times. However, when using locally produced tide tables, check carefully as they may already have been adjusted.

The second method for calculating the height of water over a wreck site is to use a tidal curve based on the tidal action for a particular area of sea. These are available from nautical almanacs and Admiralty tide tables, and are used as follows.

1. In the figure below put in the HW and LW times on the bottom row of boxes beneath the curve. The hours between can also be written in.

Using a tidal curve.

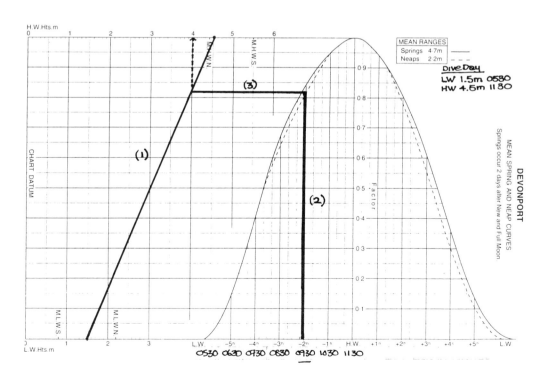

2. Note down HW and LW heights.
3. On the left hand side draw a line (1) from the bottom line marked LW for the depth given from the tide tables to the top line marked HW to the depth given from the tide tables. This is the 'tidal range' line.
4. Assume we plan to be on the dive site at 09.30. From the time boxes below the curve find 09.30 and using a ruler draw a line (2) upwards until it reaches the curved line this is the 'time' line.
5. Again using the ruler, draw another line (3) at a right angle to the time line until it meets the tidal range line (1). From the intersection of these lines, hold the ruler vertically and read from the scale on either the top or bottom lines this will give the height of water above chart datum. At the dive time 09.30 water height is 4m above chart datum: 20m + 4m = 24m.

On the tidal curve there are two curves, one marked with a continuous line, the other a broken line. The box in the top right-hand corner, 'Mean Ranges', shows that unbroken line is 'Springs' and broken line is 'Neaps'.

From the tide line (1) you have an indication of HW and LW heights and if the tide line points are near MHWS, Mean High Water Springs or MHWN, Mean High Water Neaps, then when reading the tidal curve you have an indication of whether to read the broken or unbroken curve line. With the example given, Neaps, the broken curve has been used.

Comparing the two methods we can see that the rule of twelfths table shows that actual water depth at 09.30 will be 23.75 while the tidal curve reads 4.0m above chart datum, actual depth 24m. This slight difference is because tidal curves take account of local anomalies affecting rise and fall of tides whereas the rule of twelfths is an average. Even so, the difference is only 0.25m. Tidal curves are a very quick way of finding the height above chart datum at a glance and involve less mental arithmetic than the rule of twelfths.

So the depth of water over the wreck can be estimated. Unpredictable as nature is, remember that all calculations, whether concerning earthquakes, volcanoes or tides and tidal movement, are only ever predictions.

	A 50°01'.5N 04°30'.3W		
Hours	**Rate (kn)**		
	Dir	**Sp**	**Np**
6	202	1.1	0.6
5	310	0.2	0.1
4	007	1.1	0.6
3	012	1.5	0.7
2	016	1.6	0.8
1	023	1.6	0.7
HW	029	1.3	0.6
1	031	0.6	0.3
2	203	0.5	0.2
3	197	1.1	0.5
4	196	1.8	0.4
5	198	1.7	0.8
6	203	1.3	0.6

Typical tidal diamond information found on a chart.

In addition to the height of the tide, you will also wish to know the speed and direction of any tidal movements that can be expected on your wreck at the time you plan to dive it. For this we use the tidal diamond information from a chart.

Tidal diamonds are found on a chart in a position where detailed measurements have been taken and currents relative to tidal time have been calculated. The information is displayed in a box section on the chart giving the speed of the current in knots (nautical miles per hour) and the direction in which the water flow is going for both spring (Sp) and neap (Np) tides.

Height of the Wreck above the Seabed

The depth of water over the wreck is not the only consideration when planning the dive. Wrecks lie on the seabed but, as mentioned previously, the charted depth of the wreck is to its highest point. What is the depth of the seabed? This can be found from the chart in the vicinity of the wreck. Another point to consider is the 'scour' around the hull. The scour is caused by the shifting of the seabed material by currents against and around the hull. This movement can carve out a big groove around one side of the hull. This could be a metre or more below the seabed chart datum.

The wreck in the figure above is charted at 14m. From this point there is another 15m to the seabed at chart datum of 29m and the scour increases the possible depth to 32m. The entry to the hold is at 30m. Remember that all these are chart datum figures, so the tidal height needs to be added to give true depths.

When planning dives on this wreck you would need to take account of diver experience and the

How tidal movement scours the seabed around a wreck.

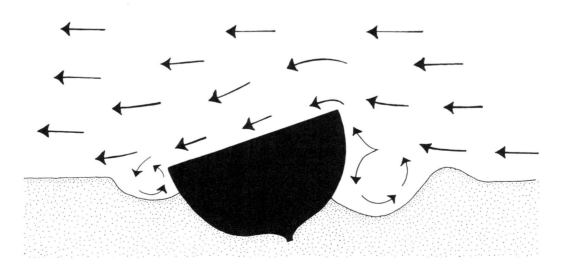

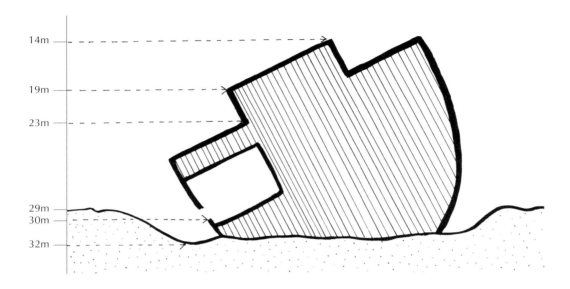

14m

19m

23m

29m
30m

32m

Wreck depths for planning a dive.

divers' optimum depth. For divers planning to enter the large hold at 30m, special care needs to be taken not to ascend too far inside the big hold as the only way out is back at 30m. Entering and ascending and then redescending gives a sawtooth dive profile, which increases the risk of decompression illness.

Many of the dive guides will publish the height the wreck stands above the seabed, which means that wreck divers can plan how deep they wish to go on a particular site. Some of the larger wrecks therefore offer quite a range of diving suited to all levels and diver interests.

Another important consideration when looking at anticipated depth are the tidal conditions on the wreck site. The movement of the tide as it floods and ebbs can in some instances be unsafe. To dive a wreck in such conditions would be extremely difficult and dangerous as you would need to hold on to something constantly to save yourself from being swept off the wreck. Undue exertion on a dive is highly undesirable as hard work increases breathing rates, depletes the air supply and greatly reduces dive time. Heavy exertion underwater is another factor that increases the risk of decompression illness.

There are some wrecks that, because of the constant heavy tidal flow, are practically undiveable. But on the majority of wrecks, there is a period of time, as tides are cyclic, when the velocity of flow must decelerate before it accelerates in the other direction. There may be little or no tidal movement at this period, which is called 'slack' water, also referred to by divers as 'the tidal window' or 'dive window'. Slack water will vary with spring or neap tides and land, and underwater features around the coastline can also affect the rate of tidal flow. Dive guides will give the best times to dive wreck sites, in the form of 'best dived 2 hours before HW, 3 hours after HW', etc. If diving a new site, local knowledge will be important to find out what tidal movement to expect.

The tidal diamonds on a chart, if near to the proposed wreck site, can also be used to find out the periods of least water movement. Reading the columns for spring or neap tides, whichever is applicable, you can see when the least water movement is by the lowest speed listed in knots.

4 How to Get to the Wreck

There are three ways you can travel to wreck dive sites: from the shore, a small boat and from a hard boat.

Wreck Diving from the Shore

Access to and from the shore line should be considered. Can the vehicle with dive kit be parked near to the shore base for the dive? If not, then a walk either carrying or wearing kit is likely. Are you and your fellow divers capable of this extra work load before entering the water? Can you manage the climb up the cliff steps with your kit after the dive?

Assuming there are no restrictions to diving from the shore, you may only need to fin out on the surface for a short distance. Taking transits or compass bearings from the shore you can locate the site and drop down onto the wreck. Alternatively, if the site is easy to locate using compass and/or pilotage using natural underwater features, you can enter the water from the shore and travel to the wreck site along the seabed.

Divers preparing for a shore dive.

44

Shore entry points can vary. Sandy beaches offer easy access but your kit will act as a magnet to sand grains! Pebble beaches give a cleaner base but, depending on their gradient, can be two steps up and one step back when getting out after the dive! Rocks may be slippery and dangerous and care should be taken. Strong wave action can tire the fittest of divers by knocking them off balance or dumping them back on the beach. Taking care, using buddy support and ensuring regulators are in the mouth should overcome problems. However, always assess the conditions and consider the entry carefully. If it looks too difficult, be safe, abort the dive.

To dive from the shore without someone acting as 'shore cover' is extremely foolhardy. Should you have any kind of problem on the dive, there is someone on the shore who can help or get help. The shore cover should be aware of the dive plan timing and you must stick to this. The shore cover should also be aware of the location of the nearest phone in case of emergencies. If shore diving is carried out by a group of divers, stagger the dive times so there are always a pair on shore to help should any problems arise.

Always remember that what may look like an easy entry at the beginning of the dive can become a difficult exit with a rising or falling tide. The local sea and weather conditions should also be carefully considered. Slight currents along the shoreline should be taken into account when heading to and from the wreck. Returning to the shore half a mile downtide of the entry point means a long walk back to your shore base unless the shore cover can use a vehicle and follow your progress!

The common sense approach is, if in doubt, don't dive.

Consider other water users in the area. You may need to take a surface marker buoy (SMB) on the wreck dive. An SMB is not normally an ideal piece of kit to use whilst diving wrecks as it can get caught on pieces of wreckage. However, most wrecks that can be reached from the shore are shallow and flattened by sea action and the SMB allows the

A surface marker buoy (SMB). The diver reels out on descent and either holds or clips on the reel – his underwater position is marked by the buoy above on the surface. Ascent is made by reeling the line in.

shore cover to know where you are at any time during the dive.

Divers should be aware of other shore users from their planned entry point. Walking through a sand castle competition in full dive kit could be regarded as a little antisocial. Entering the water alongside shore fishermen could lead to animosity and danger from flying fish-hooks. Stripping down on a beach to don dive kit might also offend if the divers get careless and bare too much! When kitting up and diving from the shore, common sense, courtesy and awareness of other shore users is important.

Wreck Diving from Small Boats

An inflatable about to be launched!

Many divers travel to wreck sites using inflatable boats or rigid inflatable boats (RIBs). These small boats have tubes full of air so are virtually unsinkable, and thus make very good diving platforms.

Inflatables can be launched without having to use slipways (as long as there are divers prepared to carry the boat and its engine to the water's edge!). Their range is generally restricted to wreck sites a few miles off or along the shore because of the optimum engine size they can carry.

RIBs are based on the same design as the inflatable but have solid hulls and, generally, must be launched from slipways or beaches where a boat trailer can be used. You need to check if you are allowed to launch and if any fees are due. RIBs usually carry high power-rated engines and electronic navigation aids, and can therefore travel greater distances than inflatables, thus widening the range of wreck dive sites within reach.

RIBs – ready and waiting for the divers to load equipment.

Both the inflatable and RIB are open boats so you need to suit up before going to sea. However, consider travel protection to and from the wreck site. No diver wants to be cold before they start a dive. Apart from being uncomfortable, cold can predispose divers to decompression illness. Even on a sunny day, a wetsuited diver and some drysuited ones can be very susceptible to wind chill whilst the boat is travelling, so windproof coats are a good idea. The body loses a lot of heat from the head and hands and a simple way to prevent this is to wear a hat and gloves. When the weather is hot, you need to be extra careful as you can still get chilled when travelling in a boat, while the effects of sunburn are often not noticed until back on shore. It is a good idea to have suitable sun screen protection and wear sunglasses to protect the eyes from the reflected glare off the water.

Launching and loading small boats in cool or warm weather can be quite hard and thirsty work, especially if suited up, and this can lead to dehydration. Dehydration, or lack of body fluids, is another factor that increases the risk of decompression sickness, so ensure that there is always a supply of soft drinks or water on board. If the weather is cold, a thermos flask with a warm drink or soup can also add greatly to your comfort.

The great thing about diving from small boats is that you do not have to carry the full weight of all the dive kit just prior to the dive. The inflatable tubes can be used to balance and fit cylinders with your diving partner's help. Once fully kitted and ready to dive, all you need do is roll off the tubes into the water.

Diver ready to roll off a RIB, holding his mask to prevent loss and holding kit that might flip upwards on entry.

make it and end up in an inelegant pose looking like a beached whale across the tubes!

No boat should go to sea unless seaworthy and carrying emergency equipment. Flares and a VHF marine radio should be carried at all times, even if the wreck site is close to shore. They can be used in case of an emergency and not just for the divers or dive boat, but on behalf of other seafarers as well. Many a dive boat has been involved in rescuing other craft or assisting with rescues.

Whether shore or small boat diving, divers should follow the divers' code of practice in letting someone ashore know where they are going, how long they will be and the expected time of return to their land base. Many divers contact the Coastguard or local harbour master to confirm their diving arrangements. They check in with the dive boat name or call sign, the numbers of divers and the proposed dive site and approximate timings. It is important to remember to contact them again at the end of diving and let them know all is well. If you forget to do this, a sea search may be instigated, wasting valuable time and money for the rescue services.

Getting back into the boat after the dive involves de-kitting at the side of the boat and passing in the weight belts and cylinder. Gripping the handles at the side of the boat and doing a bounce whilst finning hard should lift you (more or less) gracefully over the tubes. Help is always at hand if you cannot quite

Wreck Diving from Hard Boats

Hard boats of varying size are chartered for diving trips and run by a qualified skipper and crew. These boats have to conform to strict safety requirements and the skipper is responsible for the divers aboard his vessel. Most hard boats have

A small hardboat, Storm, *used for diving charters on a day basis.*

open deck space that acts as the main diving platform but may also offer the luxury of wheelhouse or cabin protection from the elements, a galley area to make hot drinks and last but by no means least, a 'head' (the nautical term for toilet).

Small dive charter boats tend to be hired on a full day basis so you need to consider suitable clothing as you will be away from land and on the open sea all day.

Some large charter boats offer on-board accommodation, meals and air fills. These 'live aboards' can be booked for diving trips to wreck sites considerable distances beyond the range of the 'day' boats.

Hardboats offer more space for divers to kit up and buddy check.

Large live-aboard hardboat, Maureen, *for diving charters.*

Dive boat skippers know the wreck sites in their working areas so liaison between them and the divers is extremely important. Great wreck diving can be achieved by considering the range of experience and interests of the divers within the group.

Stride entry from a hardboat (ladders are provided for reboarding!).

5 The Day of the Wreck Dive

Having selected a particular wreck site and planned the dive in advance, there are some further considerations to be taken into account on the dive day itself, both by the group as a whole and by each individual diver.

Group Considerations

The Water Conditions

Bad weather prior to the dive day can affect underwater visibility. For example, some wrecks lying near river mouths are best dived before high water on the incoming tide rather than after when sediment from the river flows out to sea with a falling tide. If it has been raining before the proposed dive day, this flow of river sediment obviously increases, so what might otherwise be a slightly murky dive could become a very murky dark dive.

Storms can churn the seabed near the shoreline, and silt, mud, weed and other particles may be held in suspension for some time afterwards, reducing underwater visibility.

Plankton bloom, which occurs when light levels increase after the

Bad weather prior to the dive day affected underwater visibility on this particular wreck dive.

winter months, is when marine micro-organisms multiply to such an extent that the sea can become opaque, like brown windsor or pea soup. This naturally affects underwater visibility. The sea may be very green or brown and, if the plankton accumulates in layers near the surface, it can block sunlight reaching below. The sea beneath the layers may be clear but very dark.

Storms affect not only a planned dive day but the underwater visibility as well.

Checking the weather conditions just before to the dive day can therefore give you vital information. You can contact local divers or dive shops to find out the general visibility in the area you plan to dive.

The Weather Conditions

The sea state is important to divers. It is very easy to dive from a boat into rough water and dive beneath the surface wave action. The problems arise when you surface and have to get back into a boat. The boat cover will have difficulty maintaining contact with divers on the surface as they disappear in wave troughs.

The ideal weather conditions to dive in are no wind, clear surface visibility and a flat sea surface. Unfortunately, this rarely happens, so listening to weather forecasts and learning a little basic meteorology prepares you for possibly less than ideal sea and weather conditions. Past storms far out at sea can affect a dive location with the residue wave action or swell and may preclude diving on the proposed day, even if the sun is shining and the sky is blue. Changeable weather can affect the sea state in the vicinity of the dive site very quickly. The day may begin with a reasonably calm sea but by lunchtime increasing wind strength may have caused bigger waves.

Surface visibility is another factor to consider. Rain, mist and fog reduce surface visibility for the boat cover when keeping sight of divers or their SMBs. The ability to see other boats in the near vicinity that might be a danger to the divers in the water is also reduced. To go out to sea for a sports activity when surface visibility is greatly reduced is akin to driving a car for fun on a foggy motorway!

Listening to weather forecasts on the radio and talking to the coastguard, local divers or dive shops will help you to anticipate the weather conditions to be expected on the dive site. The decision to dive must be carefully considered. Will it be safe to launch and recover a boat? Will it be safe to put divers into the sea and recover them back to the shore or boat? Will the weather remain the same for the period of travelling to, diving on and returning from the dive site?

When the sea moves up and down in waves, it can have another unfortunate effect on divers even before they reach the dive site – sea sickness! The dive site may be sheltered from wind and waves but getting there could be a rough ride in a boat. What state will everyone arrive in? Sea sickness causes dehydration, increasing the risk of decompression illness. Perhaps the proposed dive site would be better visited on another day. Do not be pushed into diving when you feel conditions, whether meteorological or personal, are not right.

There are obviously a number of important decisions to be made when diving and organizing divers and there is a need for the voice of experience within the group of divers. The answer is to nominate an organizer with diving experience as dive marshal. The dive marshal takes on the responsibility of organizing the dive, liaising with the other members of the party and ensuring that diving is carried out safely.

Time

If the slack window is tight, it might be necessary to allow more time to locate and mark the wreck site so divers can begin the dive immediately slack water begins.

Travel time depends on how far you need to go and at what speed you can travel.

The dive marshal arranges a time to meet up prior to leaving the shore. This allows divers travelling to the meeting place to plan their personal journey times. Everyone who is diving can congregate together allowing the dive marshal to check all are present and review the proposed dive plans after checking the weather and sea conditions.

The Party Members

In many instances, this is arranged before the dive day but the important points to consider are:

- Is the planned wreck depth within everyone's range?
- Are they dived up and is there the range of experience in the group to take the less experienced wreck diving?
- Are the divers fit and well on the dive day?

The dive marshal needs to know, or have allocated, who is diving with whom – the 'buddy pairs'. The reason for the wreck dive is important, Do divers want to explore, take

53

Others may be relaxing, but this dive marshal is completing the dive sheets and checking information before the next dive.

photographs or identify marine life? If there are inexperienced wreck divers in the group can they be buddied with experienced wreck divers with similar interests? A budding underwater photographer may not appreciate diving with the wreck groveller and his lump hammer!

For small boat and shore diving, the dive marshal should let someone on shore know the proposed dive site, time of departure and return, the number of people involved and type of boat and call sign, if being used.

If using a small boat, is the boat handler, the cox (abbreviation of coxswain) experienced, not just in handling the boat but also at deploying and picking up divers? In

most cases, the cox is also a diver and understands how to monitor divers when they are underwater. The cox is responsible for the boat and people in that boat, while the dive marshal, generally working with the cox, is responsible for the diving activities. If the cox decides that the safety of the boat and persons aboard are at risk, for whatever reason, the dive marshal must abide by that decision.

Hard boat diving still requires advance planning and a dive marshal to liaise with the skipper. The skipper (like the cox of a small boat) is responsible for the boat and safety of all persons aboard while the dive marshal is responsible for the organizational aspects regarding the diving procedures. Most hard boats that charter for dive groups have a skipper who, if not a diver, understands diving. Choosing a charter firm is best based on recommendation. In the absence of this, check the boat and skipper out: have they taken divers out before? If you have any doubts at all, ask around other divers or talk to the local dive clubs.

Are there divers in the group who can use emergency First Aid and oxygen equipment should a diving problem arise? Knowing who they are helps the whole group of divers,

particularly the dive marshal, if rescue skills are required.

It is obvious that the dive marshal, as the overall organizer of the dive, needs to have good organizational and interpersonal skills as well as sound working knowledge of diving procedures and safe diving practices.

The Wreck Site Itself

Is the wreck flat or upright? How far from the seabed is the main part of the wreck? What state is it in – is it so near to collapse that entry into holds

A quick sketch drawing can help divers visualize what the wreck will be like.

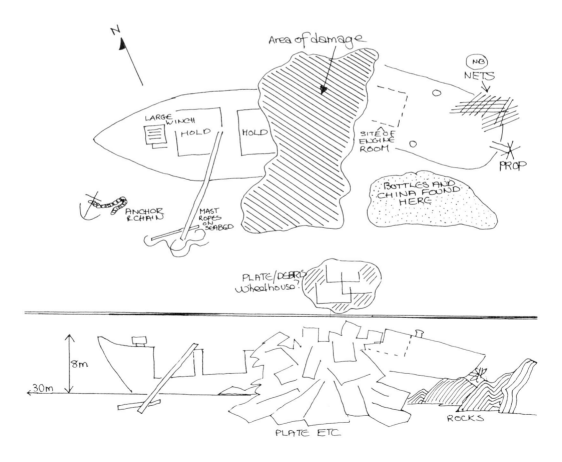

would be unwise? Are there any other dangers on the wreck, such as nets on certain areas or unexploded shells, that should be avoided?

The pre-planning of the intended dive is the stage when information on the wreck site is found out. This can then be passed on to the divers by the dive marshal to assist in helping them orientate themselves during the dive. Is the wreck easily identifiable as a ship or is it a jumble of metal with some identifiable features? Perhaps a small drawing would help the divers visualize what they are going to dive on and the best features of the wreck site.

Personal Dive Planning

Your dive plan needs to be agreed between you and the dive marshal.

Depth and Time

Dive time depends on depth and whether the time from leaving to returning to the surface includes decompression stops. Once you know the depth you intend to go to, a decompression table will give dive times according to that depth and whether decompression stops will be required. Diving computers, now much in use, can give the same type of information.

Air

You are responsible for your own air supply and you should ensure cylinders are of adequate size and configuration (*see* Chapter 9) for the proposed dive. This depends on breathing rates, depth, water temperature exertion and whether you are planning to dive around or enter a wreck where there is no direct access to the surface.

At what point should you ascend when monitoring your own and your buddy's air supply? Your breathing rate can change owing to apprehension, excitement or getting cold, so a 'reserve' (specific level) of air must be agreed, which, when reached, is the point when you and your buddy should commence your ascent even if you are well within the planned dive time. If entry into the wreck is proposed, then a safe procedure is to plan air using the 'rule of thirds'. This procedure, used by cave divers, has been adopted by wreck divers where entry into a wreck is planned. You use one third of your air in and one third out leaving the final third for emergencies.

It is a good procedure to adopt the rule of thirds even if no wreck entry is planned. You use one third of your air supply for exploration on or around the wreck, one third for the return trip and keep the remaining third for emergencies.

The dive marshal may request that you dive for a specified time. He may be taking into account slack water restrictions or how many pairs in the group can safely dive at one time. If the slack window is large and not a restriction, the dive time may be set by you with the dive marshal's agreement. However the dive time is agreed, stick to the plan. A diving slate should be kept, noting when divers left and returned to surface, their depth and decompression stops if any. The cylinder size and air before and after the dive should be noted so that if any problems arise during or after a dive, the details are to hand. Divers can also use the dive slate to transfer information into their personal dive log books when back on dry land.

The dive marshal may be diving too and if so, should appoint someone as his assistant to take over control and the dive logging while he is underwater.

6 Marking the Wreck Site

A shot line marks the site and is used by divers as the quickest route to the wreck from the surface.

Once the position of the wreck is found, it needs to be marked clearly with something that is easy to find on the surface and connected to the wreck. The marker will be used by divers as the quickest route from the surface down to the wreck and indicates the area over which the boat cover must keep watch to ensure no other surface traffic interferes.

Simple Shot Lines

A shot line is a much-used method of marking the site and one that is completely independent of the boat once deployed. The boat can, therefore, move immediately to attend to divers should they surface away from the site.

Construction

Shot lines are constructed using a large floating object, a buoy or container, to which a line is attached. The line needs to be slightly longer than the distance from the wreck to the surface. On the other end of the line, a large shot weight or 'sinker' is firmly attached.

The buoy or container at the top of the shot line should be large enough to be clearly visible on the surface. A bright colour that stands out against the sea surface colour is recommended. The surface marker needs a stout attaching point for the line, whether using a knot or a metal clip (karabiner). The buoy or container should be buoyant enough to support the weight of the line, the shot weight and partial weight of divers using the shot line as their route down to the wreck. In fact, it should be half as buoyant again so that if it does move off a wreck over deeper water it will not disappear from the surface! The principle is that 1 litre of air at the surface will support 1kg. A 25 litre plastic container will therefore support 25kg, so if a 30kg shot weight is used and the wreck is deeper than anticipated, the weight will pull the container underwater!

The Line

The line should be strong enough to support the shot weight and any strain against it, by divers or tidal movement. Nowadays, even quite thin synthetic lines have high safe working loads. However, the shot line needs to be thick enough for divers to hold easily and comfortably when descending or ascending and for handling when retrieving the shot at the end of diving. Therefore, the diameter of the rope should not be less than 30mm. Another advantage of using synthetic line is that it comes in a variety of colours, as it

To make up a shot line you need a large floating object, line and shot weight or 'sinker'.

can be quite comforting for divers to see it clearly underwater.

A simple shot line should be long enough to reach from the surface to the wreck with an additional couple of metres for attaching the shot weight, the buoy and an allowance for minor depth discrepancies. Keeping the line as near vertical as possible means divers travel the shortest route from surface to the wreck. If the line is too long it will settle at an angle and the travel distance for the divers will be greater. Too short a line means the buoy will lift the weight and 'bounce' it, more than probably off the wreck site! When using a simple shot, you have to know the depth to put the correct length of line together for the shot. There are some modifications that can be made to shot lines to compensate for rise and fall of the tide and for decompression requirements and these are discussed later in this chapter.

The Shot Weight

The shot weight, or sinker, should be heavy enough to sink and stay on the wreck site and not be lifted by the buoy on the surface, whether by wave action or moved by currents. 'Shot' in the past meant lead shot and most shot weights are lead, which has an excellent weight to volume ratio. A heavy lead shot, because of its density, is relatively small and does not take up too much room in a boat.

Other materials can be used to perform the function of a shot weight such as large iron bolts and shackles, but size and ease of handling need to be considered. The main feature of the shot is that once deployed, it should not move under the strain of use. Tide or wind action on the line and buoy, divers pulling themselves down the line or using the shot line to run additional lines from once underwater – all increase loading on the shot. The weight should be sufficient for the planned dive: in most cases around 25kg should be enough but a heavier shot may be required if deploying it prior to the 'diving window' or slack water.

Knots

Knots (if used) on a shot line must be secure. There is nothing worse for a pair of divers than descending to a wreck and suddenly finding that they are holding onto slack, wafting line with the bottom end rising up to meet them! A strong knot should be used to secure the line to the surface buoy; a bowline is ideal, whether used directly to attach the line to the buoy or to create a loop for a karabiner attachment. If the buoy connection fails, divers may well meet the surface end of the rope halfway up on the ascent while the boat monitors a drifting buoy!

The connection to the main shot can be by a bowline or an anchor bend, also known as the fisherman's bend, which can be further secured with a couple of half hitches and/or by opening the lay of the rope and threading the end of the line through the rope's tension which will 'bite' down on the threaded end.

Knots for Shots – the Bowline

1. *Make a loop in the line.*

2. *Pass the end back through the loop.*

3. *Pass the end behind the line and back down through the loop.*

4. *Tighten the knot by pulling on the line.*

Knots for Shots – the Anchor Bend

1. *Make two turns with the end of the line around a ring.*

2. *Pass the end in front of the main line and through the turns and tighten – this is the fisherman's bend.*

3. *Next, with the end of the line make a loop over the main line, pass the end underneath and back through the loop. (A half hitch, or to sewers, blanket stitch!)*

4. *Make another half hitch to finish off.*

A buoy connected by a bowline, shot weight connected by an anchor bend, half hitches and threading end through main line (right). The end is threaded through the rope, which will bite down under tension (left).

Preparing the Shot Line

Some dive boats carry lines pre-measured to 10m, 15m, 20m, 30m, and so on, and use a line that is slightly longer than the anticipated depth, shortening it if necessary in their shot preparation. A chain sinnet is quite an effective way of keeping the shortening process neat on a line too long for the depth required. Another method is to tie off the line in loops and secure to the buoy. Loops of line can entangle divers so the loops should be tied neatly or put in a bag hung below the buoy.

If only shorter lines are available they can be joined together to give the correct length. This needs a knot that will hold securely but be easy to undo at the end of diving, and for this a bowline is ideal. However, with proper planning you should know the depth of the dive, and a single line of the right length is always the best option.

Lines have an in-built tendency to loop and knot themselves unless they are carefully tended. The storing, deploying and retrieval of shot lines needs careful consideration. There is nothing worse than sitting in a dive boat with metres of line haphazardly lying around. Dive kit and divers can get caught up, and trying to deploy the shot, line and buoy then becomes a dangerous exercise. Create a clear area or contain the shot line, buoy and weight in a basket, box or, when using plastic drums, around the drum itself.

Chain sinnets shorten the line.

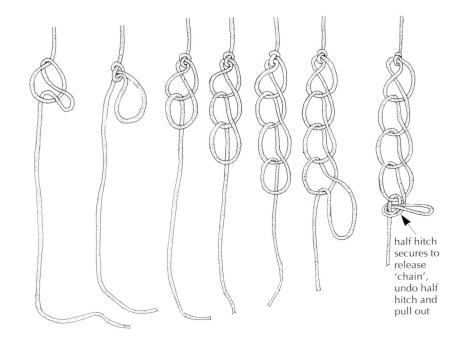

half hitch secures to release 'chain', undo half hitch and pull out

Two bowlines used to join shorter lines into one shot line.

For small-boat wreck diving, the shot line can be prepared before leaving the shore, as trying to do so at sea while contending with the effect of wave action on the boat can be interesting! First make the buoy and shot weight attachments. Feed the line carefully in open loops ('flaking' the line) onto clear deck space or into the container or basket. The important thing here is to remember to feed in the buoy end of the line first and finish with the shot weight laid on the top – remember the shot end is deployed first into the water!

If you are using the drum type of buoy, the line can be wrapped around it and secured off at the shot weight end so it does not unravel until needed. The loop can be released just before use so the line will run out as soon as the drum and shot are deployed. The shot spins the line off the drum as it descends.

Where space allows, the line can be flaked in preparation for 'no tangle' shot deployment.

Flaking the shot line into a basket. Remember to feed the buoy end in first and finish with the shot weight, as this is deployed first!

Winding the shot line onto the drum container. Patience and long arms are needed.

The line secured with a loop so it does not unravel.

When an echo sounder is being used on a boat, the transducer is fixed to or is located in the boat's hull. The transducer is the part of the sounder system that sends and receives ultrasonic waves down to the seabed. If the transducer is situated to one side of a boat, this is the best place to deploy the shot when the echo sounder picks up the wreck site. The transducer could be sited closer to the stern of the boat, so that deploying the shot in the 'working area' of the boat is then possible.

When deploying shot lines, it is very important to ensure the boat's turning propeller does not come into contact with the line. If the engine is put into neutral the propeller does not turn, so there is no risk of entanglement as the shot is deployed. Another method is to stay under power and circle the descending shot. When circling around, the stern is pushing away

Once the shot is deployed, the line spins off the drum.

from the centre and a moving prop will not get tangled.

The person deploying the shot prepares in advance by laying the shot weight on the tubes of a small boat or the gunwales (sides above the deck) of a large boat. He ensures that the line is clear of any obstructions, including people, and that the large buoy is free to go into the water as the line pays out.

Deploying

The order to deploy the shot must be pre-arranged between the skipper/cox and the shot deployer, and is given by the skipper/cox, who is monitoring the transits, the echo sounder or the electronic navigation aids, when he can 'see' the site and puts the engine into neutral. The shot deployer throws the shot weight first, allows the line to 'flake out' and then throws the buoy clear

of the boat. The shot weight sinks, taking the line down almost instantly, and reaches the wreck very quickly. You should never try to hand feed the shot down through the water. The weight is too heavy to control safely, and by the time it reaches the seabed it will, in all probability, be some way from the site because of the boat's drift on the surface. Once the shot is in position, it should be checked by using position-fixing methods to ensure that it is not moving off site by dragging (because is too light or too short).

The best shot deployment is directly onto the wreck. However, time and tide can place the shot beside or near the wreck. Knowing what the wreck looks like on an echo sounder, how it lies on the seabed for example, bows to the west, stern to the east and what the tide is doing, makes it easier to make a sound judgement.

Heading into the tidal stream and deploying the shot as soon as the

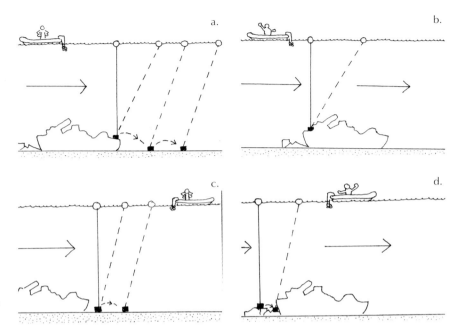

a. Heading into the tidal stream and deploying shot as soon as the wreck 'shows' on echo sounder may mean shot being moved off the wreck.

b. Heading into the tidal stream and deploying shot when the wreck 'falls away' on echo sounder keeps shot on the wreck.

c. Drifting with the tidal stream and deploying shot when the wreck 'falls away' on echo sounder may mean shot being moved off the wreck.

d. Drifting with the tidal stream and deploying shot as soon as the wreck 'shows' on echo sounder keeps shot on the wreck.

wreckage shows on the echo sounder may mean the shot ends up on the downtide side of the wreck, as the boat may drift back a little when engines are put into neutral. If the shot is not heavy enough the buoy may lift the shot and with wave action and current, 'bounce' it away from the wreck. Waiting a little after the wreck shows on an echo sounder until it begins to fall away again and then shotting may place the shot on the wreck or uptide of it. If the shot is uptide and does move for some reason, the chances are that it will jam into the side of the wreckage and be very secure. Remember this when retrieving the shot; pulling it up may prove difficult and motoring further uptide may be necessary to get enough angle on the line to release the weight.

It is also quite feasible to shot by drifting with the tide and releasing the shot as soon as the wreck shows on the echo sounder. The shot should end up uptide or on the wreck. If you leave it too late the shot will end up in a downtide position and may be moved away from the site.

Shots can be deployed by just using transits without the use of echo sounders. However, keep an eye on the tidal direction and the wind. When the boat's engine goes into neutral the boat may drift slightly and the shotting may be off the transits and, therefore, off the wreck site! There is a very well-known wreck that appears almost everywhere where divers dive known as 'HMS Vicinity'! Most divers have dived this wreck at one time or another.

Once the shot line has been deployed and checked, the divers can kit up, buddy check and be dropped off by the boat near to the

shot. Unless the water movement is truly slack, the boat should drop the divers uptide of the shot so they can drift onto it. Dropping the divers downtide means they have to swim against the tide to reach the shot and disgruntled sounds may be heard as they struggle against the tidal movement!

Watching how the line descends from the buoy indicates which way the tide is moving; the buoy will always be downtide of the shot weight position. If divers are dropped uptide they can drift back onto the shot.

Another way to monitor the tidal movement is to put another small

A happy diver – on the shot without any effort!

The tide indicator streaming downtide of the main buoy means the divers need to be dropped off uptide so they drift onto the buoy.

Tide indicator on a shot buoy. The slack line shows there is no tidal movement.

buoy (variously called tide indicator, monkey's tail, tide tail or flow marker) on a short line and attach this to the main shot buoy. This small buoy and line will stream out downtide from the main buoy. This means that divers can be dropped uptide with the tide marker and main buoy 'in transit' and drift directly onto the shot. If the line on the tide indicator is not taut, then there is little or no tidal movement and the water is 'slack'.

'On the Wreck' Signals

Most divers know what it is like to dive *HMS Vicinity*! There is often insufficient time to wait for the first pair of divers to report whether the shot was on the planned site or not. The first pair may descend and, not finding the shot on the wreck, carry out a search before ascending and reporting lack of wreckage. Some form of communication from them

to indicate that they have landed on the wreck is a good idea.

If the shot is on the wreck and it is not too deep, pulling on the shot line a couple of times will make the surface buoy bounce up and down. This is a good idea in principle but people on the boat may not be able to distinguish a series of agreed pulls from wave action.

A better 'we are on the wreck' signal is for the first pair of divers to take down with them an uncrushable small container (a lavatory ballcock is ideal, or fisherman's small pot marker). The ball is attached to the shot line by a small line and karabiner, large enough to run smoothly up the line. (Obviously, this will not work on joined lengths of line, it needs one single shot line.) If the shot is on the wreck, the buoy can be released, its buoyancy taking it to the surface while still connected by the running line to the shot line. When it bobs up on the surface by the shot buoy it signals 'Shot on wreck'. If it

A washball connected to shot line with a large karabiner to allow smooth ascent up the line.

The washball is clear to run up to surface.

doesn't appear it means the shot is off the wreck and the decision to dive or not by the rest of the group can be made. This 'wreck indicator' is known by many names, including washball, wreckball, and 'go-ball'.

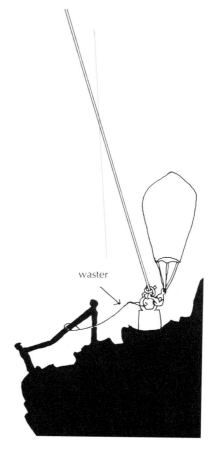

A waster used to connect the shot weight to the wreck.

A lift bag on a shot weight makes recovery easier from the surface.

After the Dive

Retrieving the shot back to the boat by heaving on the line need not be hard work. Large boats usually have a motor winch so that the shot line and weight can be retrieved easily. For small boats without winches, the last pair of divers to ascend or use the shot can attach a lift bag to the shot. The lift bag is carefully filled so that it is not quite buoyant. The divers, if ascending, need to ensure they do not pull on the shot line. If the last pair of divers are not returning to the shot, they partially fill the bag and leave it.

Once the divers are back in the boat or clear of the shot on their dive, the shot line can be retrieved. With a gentle tug, given either manually or by the boat going astern with the shot line attached inboard, the lift bag will rise, the air inside it expands and the weight is brought to the surface. Care is needed to coil in the shot line and retrieve the weight. If the lift bag tips and loses its air, the

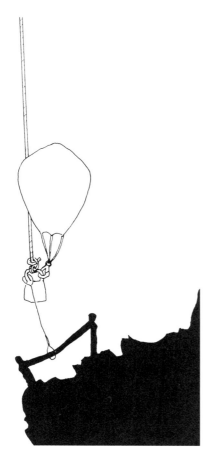

The lift bag is lifting the shot weight clear from the wreck but is still connected by the waster.

part of the wreck. They connect and fill a lift bag to move the weight off the wreck. The lift bag can then be filled a little more so that the waster is taut. The remaining divers descend and ascend the shot line as normal. At the end of diving, the shot line can be pulled away from the wreck by using the boat's engine power. The pull from the surface will break the waster and the lift bag will bring the shot to the surface away from the boat.

Other Types of Shot Line

There are always variations on a theme and shot lines too can be varied to suit conditions and the type of dive.

Double-weighted Shot Line

There is one method of double shot weights that can be used for small wreck sites, such as submarines. The shot is made up using two shot weights, one at the end of the line as normal and the other at some distance from the end. The first shot is deployed, the line flakes out and with a slight time delay takes the second shot down. The line continues flaking out until the buoy can be thrown. Part of the shot line is now a fixed ground line, a jackstay, between the two shots and lies across the small site. Having descended the shot line, the divers can use the jackstay as a base to search and locate the small wreck. With this double shot system, remember to allow enough line to

shot will descend once more and the line should be free to run out (still with the buoy attached). Recovering the lift bag carefully should ensure that this won't happen.

Another way of ensuring that the weight does not become snagged when being lifted from a wreck is to use a 'waster' line. The shot is set up and deployed using buoy, line and weight. The divers descend and attach a low-breaking-strain line, the waster, from the shot to a secure

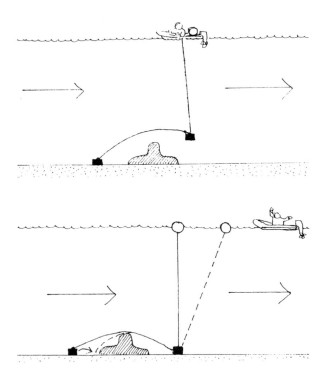

Counterweight or Pendulum Shot

Top-tensioned Lines

A top-tensioned shot line is useful where surface position fixes are being taken the pulley effect straightening the shot line almost vertically above the shot on the wreck site below. A boat can come alongside the buoy and, using electronic navigation aids, compass bearings or transits, can fix or check the wreck site position.

A top-tensioned shot uses the same components as a simple shot: buoy, line, shot weight but with the addition of a small counterweight or pendulum weight. The line needs to be long enough to allow for anticipated depth, tide and current. Instead of attaching the top of the line to the buoy as usual, run it through the attaching point of the buoy. This should be large enough to allow the line to run through freely. The free end of the line is then attached to a small counterweight. The line runs

After laying the first shot, the boat drifts back, or goes astern, to drop the second shot (upper). The double shots deployed over the wreck site (lower).

reach the bottom with the second shot and form the jackstay to the first shot. Placing lift bags on each shot at the end of diving assists with recovery back to the boat.

A top-tensioned shot reduces the angle and shortens the travel distance.

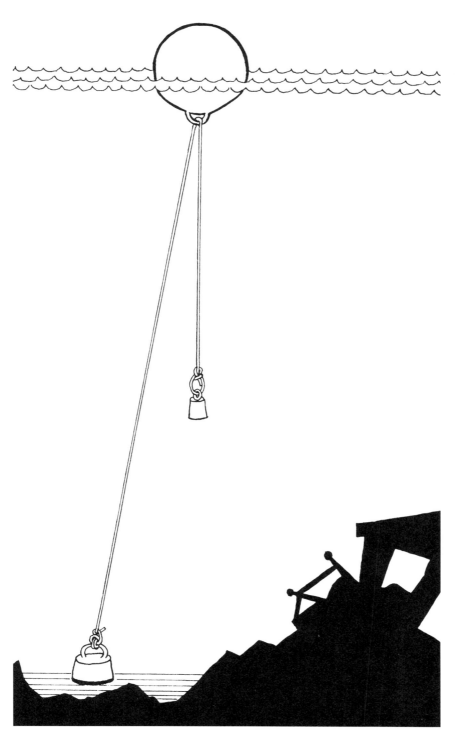

The top-tensioned shot: the small pendulum counter weight acts as the line tensioner.

The drum with the line running free through the handle and a counterweight attached to the end using a bowline (left). A 'clog' linking the two lines together but allowing free movement (right).

through the buoy attachment with the counterweight maintaining tension on the main line, which falls in a straighter line down to the wreck.

There can be problems with this type of pendulum shot. Deployment needs to be carefully controlled because throwing the buoy with the counterweight at the same time as the shot weight may cause the counterweight to spin and tangle around the main shot line, preventing it from reaching the wreck site. To avoid this, throw the main shot first and allow the line to flake out before deploying the buoy and counterweight together.

Another problem with counterweight shots is that if too much line is used the counterweight will hang down some way and the line to it can be mistaken for the main shot line. Divers have been known to descend to what they thought was the wreck and finding instead a weight and clear water below them!

This problem of identifying the main shot line can be resolved by having some means of keeping the two lines together but allowing free running without entanglement. A 'clog' (found in climbing stores) can be used feed the shot line through one eye before running it through

the buoy attachment and feed the line back through the other eye before attaching the counterweight. The lines are then together but still free to move.

A simple, large karabiner can also be used to keep the lines together. Another method is to use a counterweight with a large eye; a shackle of sufficient weight can then be used to connect the two lines together while again allowing free running of the lines.

An important fact to consider is that we have created a pulley system. This will cause the counterweight to reduce the effectiveness of the main shot. Also, more critically, the buoy will be pulled down with a force equivalent to twice the weight of the counterweight. For example, a 10-litre buoy will support 10kg. If the counterweight weighs 5kg, the pulley effect will put a strain of 10kg on the buoy! The buoy needs to support twice the weight of the counterweight, plus the line and an allowance for the effect of tide. The bigger the buoy the better. Working on the principle that the counterweight is a sixth of the weight support of the buoy should give the desired result.

A large karabiner connecting the counterweight to the shot line, allowing free movement of both lines (left). A large, heavy D ring counterweight allowing free movement of both lines (right).

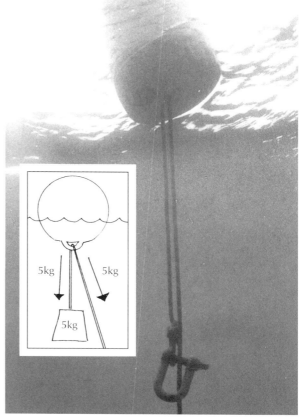

Bottom-Tensioned Lines

Another type of pendulum shot is one that uses the other end of the shot line: a bottom-tensioned shot. This uses the pulley effect in reverse. The shot line is passed through the handle of a large kara-biner or shackle attached to the shot, allowing free movement of the line. The end of the line is then attached to a connector and a lifting bag. The connector should be large enough not to pass back through eye of the shot connector. The lift-ing bag is partially filled to tension the line. As with the top-tensioned shot the key thing to remember is the pulley effect created, this time by the lift bag on the shot. If the bag contains 5 litres of air, this equals 5kg of lift and, with the pulley effect, this equates to 10kg tension on the shot. Remember the 'one sixth' weight ratio rule to ensure a heavy enough shot weight.

Top-tensioned shot lines are easi-er to set up in that the line can be deployed all in one go from the sur-face in controlled conditions. The bottom-tensioned shot requires the divers who fill the bag to ensure they don't put too much air in the lift bag. It might be a good idea for the bag or plastic container to be marked to indicate the fill line in relation to the shot weight.

Some divers use tensioned shot lines all the time because they allow for the rise and fall of the tide, and keep the line straighter and therefore provide the most direct way down to the wreck. Are these perhaps excus-es for not planning and preparing buoys, lengths of line and sufficient weight for the planned dive?

The important thing to remember is that tensioned shots, by their very nature, have a line that moves. Divers who rely on holding onto shot lines or who like to hold a steady line, will find themselves holding on but either moving up or down with the line. Their weight affects the counterbalance system, and wave action at the surface causes the buoy with either type of counterweight to rise and fall and consequently move the line. This must be considered if decompres-sion is planned for the dive using a shot line. Trying to maintain a 'stop' depth with a moving line could compromise a diver's safety.

Anchor Lines

You may have, or will come across, a method of marking a wreck site that uses the boat's anchor line. This method is not recommended for reasons detailed below and is not used by many professional skippers.

A boat's anchor, anchor chain and line can be lowered so that when the anchor is snagged in the wreck, the boat drifts back but remains held on station above the wreck. Divers kit up, enter the water from the boat and use the anchor line for their descent and ascent from the wreck. With the boat at the top of the anchor line, little swim-ming on the surface is necessary before getting back into the boat.

The boat, held by the anchor, is affected by wind and tide and this can put enormous strain via the anchor line on the wreckage the

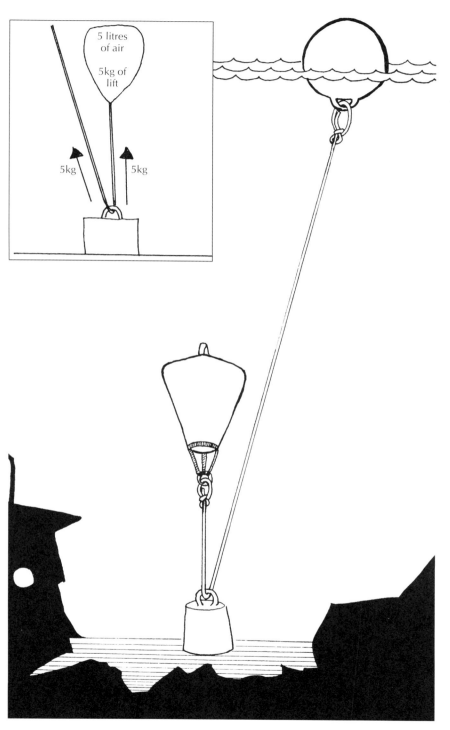

5 litres
of air

5kg of
lift

5kg

5kg

The bottom-tensioned shot: the air bag acts as the line tensioner. The pulley effect of the lift bag on the shot needs consideration to ensure the shot is heavy enough to remain on the wreck.

anchor is holding to. Wreckage can be lifted or broken away, and this damage may weaken surrounding wreck structure. If divers are in the near vicinity, this is dangerous. A choppy sea can make the anchor line 'snatch' and relax. Divers descending or ascending need to stay clear but close to the line and, if there is a current, holding the anchor line can be uncomfortable. Carrying out decompression or safety stops could also be compromised by having to hold onto the anchor line.

The other main problem of anchoring into a wreck is if divers ascend in some other way than up the anchor line. They may then need to be picked up by the boat and it will have to move off station quickly if the divers have any kind of a problem. There may be other divers underwater returning to or commencing their ascent up the anchor

line, so to pull the anchor would be dangerous in this situation.

When a boat anchor is being used to mark the site it needs to have a buoy attached. If the boat has to move, the anchor line is released and the buoy supports the line end on the surface. The method of release needs to be easy and quick, bearing in mind that the boat held by its anchor puts quite a strain on the line. The engine will need to be started and the boat manoeuvred forward to release the buoy and all this has to be done before the divers can be attended to. If the divers have a serious problem there can be a potentially dangerous time delay in reaching them with this method of marking a wreck site.

The potential safety hazards caused by anchoring into a wreck and the damage anchors cause wreckage mean that this practice is not recommended.

7 Decompression

A deeper wreck dive may be planned to include decompression stops. The shot line can be used for the placement of a 'decompressing station'.

Marking Decompression Stops

A simple decompression stop mark can be made on the line by measuring the required distance from the attaching point at the buoy and marking the stop depth with insulating tape. The divers can check their 'decompression stop' depth as they near the taped mark as it indicates the 'stop' area on the line.

Other methods can be used to mark a decompression stop. A short line of a different colour to the shot line can be threaded through at the required depth. This idea can be extended so that the smaller line forms loops so divers can hang from the loops rather than gripping a straight line.

Another method is to make a fixed loop at the decompression stop point. Divers can then clip off to this with a small line, sometimes called a hang line, and pull away from the shot line. Care is needed here to maintain the correct decompression depth with good buoyancy control and firm hold on the hang line. This system allows divers to decompress out of the way of other divers descending while still maintaining contact with the shot line. A useful loop knot is the dropper knot (or artilleryman's hitch). It can be tied underwater if the line is not too taut and is very easy to release when no longer needed.

Tape marks the shot line at decompression stops. There is also a small loop through the main line for a hang line connection.

81

Divers decompressing using the hang line from a dropper knot, allowing decompression to be clear of descending divers.

Dropper Knot or Artilleryman's Hitch

1. Make a loop in the line.

2. Flop it over so the main line is at the back.

3. Pull one side of the loop under the main line.

4. Pull the loop through, which tightens the knot.

A clog fixed as loop connector in shot line for the 'hang line' to be connected.

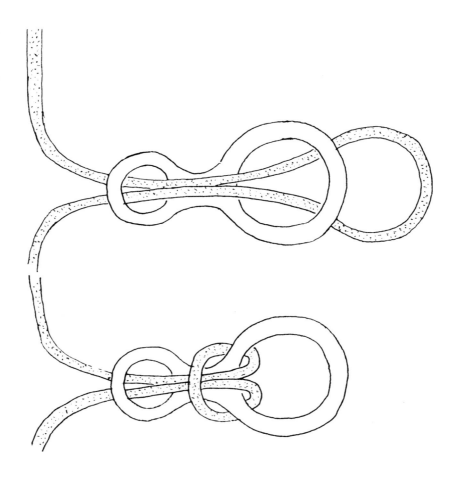

An alternative to the loop is to connect a 'clog' on the line. As with the dropper knot it needs a little slack in the line to set but, again, can easily be removed.

A second line can be attached to the shot buoy, measured so that a spare cylinder will hang from it at the decompression stop depth. If there is then any problem with retrieving the shot line, the spare cylinder can still be easily retrieved as it is not attached to the main shot line. This spare cylinder is a 'fail safe' in case decompressing divers run short on their own air supply, which might happen occasionally even though divers should rely on their own air supply to complete the dive back to the surface. The spare cylinder caters for divers who may have worked and breathed harder than they anticipated on the dive or gone beyond planned dive times or maximum planned depth. The divers may have to remain at a decompression stop longer than they originally planned.

The line with the cylinder and two regulators can be attached to the shot buoy after the shot has been deployed. The cylinder

Spare cylinder hung from shot buoy and a link line connecting it to the main shot line for divers to use on ascent.

*A non-tidal
separation
scheme for a
decompression
station.*

link line

should be left turned off so it does not accidentally 'free flow' during deployment. Should divers need to use it they can turn the air on. The spare cylinder can only be used if the divers return to the surface via the shot line. If a spare cylinder is set up it should be pointed out to the diving group that it is an emergency supply and its use should not be included when calculating the air supply for a dive plan.

Separation Schemes for Decompressing Divers

To decompress on a shot line that may be busy with divers descending and ascending at the same time may cause a congestion problem. To hang away from the main shot line on an additional line prevents collisions but decompressing in a stream of rising bubbles from other divers below can cause disorientation and possibly slight loss of buoyancy. If the shot line is going to be busy then a down-and-up-diver separation scheme can resolve the problem.

One separation scheme for nontidal conditions is where the spare cylinder, rather than being attached from the main shot buoy, has its own surface buoy. The cylinder is set on a line at the required decompression stop depth. Below the cylinder the line is kept tensioned by using a small weight. Another line is attached at the weight point preferably a different colour to the shot line or colour coded with tape which has a karabiner connection that clips

around the shot line. The karabiner should be heavy enough or weighted so it can run freely down the main shot line. The cylinder is now connected to the main shot line by the link line. The link line should be long enough to run sideways and upwards to the cylinder line.

The ascending divers reach the link line on the shot line and fork off to the decompression stop cylinder. They can then complete their decompression stops without diver traffic interference and then return to the surface on the decompression station buoy.

The decompression station line, buoy and cylinder attachment can be deployed after the main shot from the surface. Connecting the link line karabiner around the top of the shot line will allow the link line to descend the shot line. Attached to the other end of the link line, the weight, line with cylinder attached and the buoy can be carefully deployed into the water. The decompression station buoy will drift away from the main buoy but be held to it by the link line. The cylinder can be turned on underwater by the first pair of divers if required.

If the tide turns, problems with this separation scheme may arise. The tidal movement will pull the decompression station buoy away from the main buoy and the straightening line will lift the link line karabiner up the shot line. Divers ascending might find themselves having to go higher than the desired decompression stop depth. To allow the decompression station to drift with tide away from the shot, the link line needs to be disconnected; divers doing so would

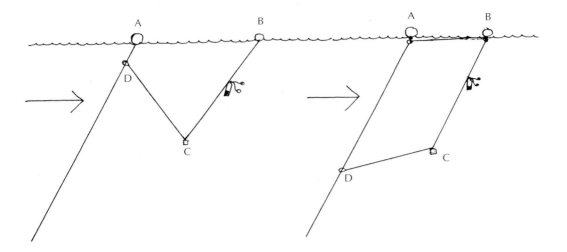

Tidal movement has pulled the decompression station away from the main shot line and lifted link line connection D up the shot line (left). The additional line between buoys A and B on the surface prevents link line connection D lifting (right).

then find the cylinder sinking back to the required depth. However, a re-descent at the most critical part of the divers' ascent is dangerous practice.

If the slack window is tight and the last pair of divers expect more tidal movement than others who dived before, an addition needs be made to the separation scheme to ensure that the divers are not forced to re-descend to the decompression station.

An additional line is attached to the buoy connections on the surface. When the last pair of divers ascend up the link line to arrive at C, they unclip the link line before ascending to the decompression stop. The surface cover should be able to see their bubbles by the decompression shot and can release the surface line holding the decompression buoy to the main buoy. If bubble sighting on the surface could be a problem then a signal from the decompressing divers needs to be given to the surface

cover to unclip the surface connection. A mini washball (see Chapter 6, page 71) can be attached at a point near the cylinder so that when the divers reach it they release the washball up the cylinder line to the surface to indicate that they are 'on station' and that the surface line can be released. Once the decompression station buoy is disconnected from the main shot buoy the whole station, with the divers carrying out required decompression stops, can drift with the tide. This is far more comfortable that trying to maintain a hold on a fixed line against the tidal movement known as being a 'flag'. The decompression buoy on the surface marks the divers' position for the boat cover to maintain contact and pick up the divers when they surface.

Another variation on this theme of the link line separation scheme is to use more cylinders by setting them on a weighted bar at the required decompression stop. The bar is supported at the required depth by

The weighted bar decompression station.

being suspended beneath two buoys on lines at either end. A link line is clipped to one end of the bar and to the main shot line. Again, this works best in non-tidal conditions, so should the window be tight, adaptations will need to be made as before to ensure that the link line does not get pulled higher than the desired decompression stop depth.

Any setting of a decompression station at a measured depth depends upon a reasonably flat sea surface. If this is not the case, the station buoys move up and down with the wave action and the station will move likewise. Divers should always check their stop depth and be prepared to decompress slightly above or below a station. The rise and fall should be small so that the diver can adapt his position to remain at the correct depth if the station does move slightly without too much difficulty.

8 Diving the Wreck

What should divers prepare themselves for when diving and exploring a wreck?

Wreck Exterior

Overall Good Visibility

Wreck lying at an angle on the seabed.

Even with good visibility, depending upon the state and age of the wreck, it may be difficult to identify exactly where you are. The wreck may be lying at an acute angle or on its side.

A good description or sketch of the wreck and some knowledge of ship construction will help in identifying the general area being dived. If the wreck is on its side the simplest thing to do to orientate yourself is to tip sideways to make recognition easier.

You will also need to take into account the marine life that has taken over the wreck. Marine growth will alter the shape of ship parts

quite dramatically so you may fin past something without realizing what it is. The clue is to look for shapes that don't quite fit in with the surrounding sea life: man-made items with a straight line or a perfect curve. With practice, you will begin to realize what lies beneath.

The metal will be rusty and wood split so there will be sharp edges to avoid. Where metal has rusted, a layer of orange-brown dust will, if brushed against, rise up and cover you so you look like part of the wreck! Silt may well cover the outside of a wreck, and if disturbed, will lower visibility. Good buoyancy control and slow gentle movements will be needed to prevent disturbance of these particles. Fins are the main culprit: keep finning action to a minimum and keep your legs bent with the fins slightly higher than your knees, which should prevent too much disturbance. If you need to move along a piece of wreckage, use the finger walking technique as this saves on finning action. Your buoyancy control is also important to avoid sharp edges that have a rather detrimental effect on dive suits!

Ropes may be entangled in and around the wreck and need to be avoided to prevent snagging. On some wrecks, fishing nets and lines can cause the same problem.

A wreck might be in a state of collapse, so the potential risk of movement underneath pieces of loose wreckage outside the wreck should be assessed carefully. As soon as you fin beneath wreckage or overhangs, you are diving 'no clear surface', meaning that direct ascent is impossible. Always check

first. Is it stable? Is it large enough to fin through or under? Is there a visible entry and exit point? Will it be easy to clear the overhang? Will finning through or underneath reduce visibility?

Parts of wreckage may be recognizable – here the diver is in front of a ship's boiler.

Overall Poor Visibility

Diving a wreck in low visibility is not many divers' idea of fun. However, if you do decide to do a wreck dive where overall visibility is reduced, the techniques described in the next chapter will be useful.

91

Inside the Wreck

Penetrating the wreck means entering the main body of the ship, its hull and superstructure. You may be able to penetrate the holds vertically or horizontally, especially when the decking or hatches have collapsed or disappeared and damage to the hull offers large entry/exit points. Quite often this type of penetration, where only the main deck beams are left, provides wonderful diving. The holds offer protection for fish life and with only the skeleton of the main deck above, light penetrates easily. This might not necessarily create a 'no clear surface' situation but you must always remember where you are as it is easy to stray into covered areas without realizing that the surface has become obscured.

(Above) A diver checking 'what's underneath?'

Diver in the skeleton of a wreck.

Diver checking entry point into the wreck.

If plans of the ship are available, you can use these to orientate yourself during the dive. You do need to remember, however, that the plans were drawn up for the vessel when it was built and this may have been some time in the past. A lot has happened to it since then, including becoming a wreck!

Penetration into large areas with easy entry and exit points may be possible. For wreck 'caverns' remember to monitor your depth carefully so you don't exceed your

Diver moving very carefully through part of a wreck.

planned maximum depth or ascend too much inside if your only way out is back down at depth. You always need to be aware of where you are and how far you are from your entry point, which may be easy to see with light conditions outside the wreck. The inside of the wreck will be silty or rusty so, as on the outside, good buoyancy control and slow gentle movements will be needed to prevent reducing the visibility. Your bubbles may reduce visibility as well. As they rise and get trapped against the surface above you they may lift rust or even penetrate through to silty areas above your 'ceiling' and disturb them: the result could be a fine 'rain' descending on you!

You may find air pockets, but if you surface in one, do not be tempted to remove your regulator and chat to your buddy as the air will probably be foul. Sharp edges and protruding pieces need to be manoeuvred past with care, and as room to manoeuvre may be restricted, you and your buddy cannot always explore side by side and have enough room to turn around. Some techniques described in the next chapter will help with gentle penetration diving.

Extended Wreck Penetration

Warning! Deep penetration into a wreck is akin to cave diving.

This type of wreck diving needs great care, planning and experience and, most important, commitment. Do you want to do it? If you are someone who hates tunnels and small spaces, then a 'no clear surface' deep wreck penetration dive is not for you. If you do want to do it then you should seriously consider contacting a cave diving club or experienced group of extended penetration divers and work with them to build up your knowledge, specialist skills and risk awareness. Do not assume that someone who calls himself a deep penetration diver and says he can take you for a good dive has those skills. To carry out extended penetration into a wreck you need to go on build-up dives to practise techniques and experienced buddies to work with.

To Penetrate or Not?

In some diving circles you are not deemed to be a true wreck diver if you don't like going inside wrecks. This attitude is best ignored as diving wrecks without penetration still offers the opportunity to explore, discover and enjoy the wreck. Many finds are made on and around the wreck; remember how the ship will have twisted and tilted before hitting the seabed, and how many interesting items will have slid off and are now buried in the seabed surrounding the wreck? What came out of the holds when the hull split open?

9 Air Supply

The wreck environment, as can be seen from the last chapter, needs to be taken into consideration and planned for. As divers, we always plan how much air we will require for a dive, but wreck diving needs some additional considerations.

Sharp edges are not the ideal environment for rubber hoses supplying air to you! Good buoyancy control and awareness of what is in the immediate vicinity should prevent hoses getting caught. If they do, then you should move back and carefully release the hose. A hefty tug could cause damage and subsequent loss of air!

You need to think about streamlining your equipment overall but, in particular, hoses should not be sprouting out at all angles. Hose retainer clips or Velcro straps can keep hoses close to the diver's body and reduce the 'loop' effect. There is one piece of equipment, however, that must have a quick release retainer: the diver's Alternative Air System or AAS.

Alternative Air System

The AAS is a back-up system generally considered to be for your buddy should he have a problem with his air supply, and it falls into two categories: integrated into a buoyancy jacket or 'octopus' secondary regulator.

The Buoyancy Jacket Integrated AAS

The AAS is integrated into the buoyancy jacket by combining the direct

Diver checking air supply and quick release AAS holder.

Buoyancy jacket with combined direct feed and AAS.

feed supply to the jacket with an extra second-stage regulator. This is either by complete integration with the direct feed controls, or by a 'bi-furcated' unit, where another hose and regulator are linked to the jacket's direct feed hose. Some systems use a slightly longer direct feed hose than normal when integrated units are fitted.

If a diver's buddy runs out of air in an emergency situation, this type of system has its limitations. If the

out-of-air buddy uses the completely integrated unit with its short hose, the pair will have to ascend side by side with the rescuer's buoyancy controls in the mouth of a possibly panicking diver! With the bifurcated unit, again with a short hose and its connection near the buoyancy controls, the same problems could arise.

Remember that the rescuer needs to be in total control if an out-of-air situation arises, it is he who will have

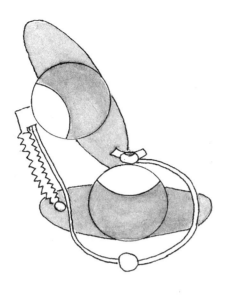

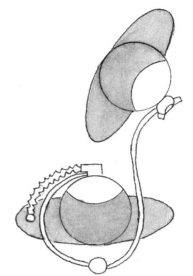

to assist his buddy to the surface. If either of these systems are used as an AAS, the rescuer should give the buddy his main regulator and use the AAS himself, thereby retaining control of buoyancy. Having to remove the primary regulator and switch to using the AAS might sound easy, but the rescuer is adding to possible problems by switching regulators and more than likely he will be approaching panic too!

The integrated and bifurcated systems really only work as a 'self-help' piece of equipment. If the diver wearing them has a problem with his primary regulator he can easily switch to either type of unit mentioned above. However, it will not help if the wearer runs out of air and his buoyancy jacket and main regulator are run from the same cylinder!

There is also a system where, if the main air supply is depleted, the integrated system automatically switches to allow the diver to breathe via the jacket using the emergency air cylinder. This is an extension of the self-help idea, but should be regarded only as a last resort.

The Octopus AAS

If we are looking at the ideal AAS requirements, quick deployment with the rescuer controlling the emergency easily, retaining his own air supply and room for the buddy pair to face each other or fin side by side, the octopus AAS is the best option.

An octopus is a spare regulator added to the diver's first stage so the rescuer does not have to remove his own regulator. The hose, longer than a standard regulator hose, allows room for the rescuer and buddy to keep hold of each other. If necessary they can fin side by side to a point of straight ascent to the surface. They can adjust position for the ascent so

Divers on octopus, side by side.

Divers on octopus, finning side by side.

that they face each other and, keeping hold so the hose does not get pulled, they can ascend.

With the octopus you do need to consider a number of points. Firstly, which side should it be mounted on? There are many different views about whether an octopus should be mounted on a diver's right or left side. This can depend on configuration of the diver's kit but 'is it effective?' is the main question to ask.

Divers on octopus, static and face to face prior to ascent.

Divers on octopus, face to face on ascent.

(Left) Right-handed octopus run over left shoulder of rescuer. (Right) Right-handed octopus run over left shoulder of rescuer will have hose kink if buddy takes rescuer's primary regulator.

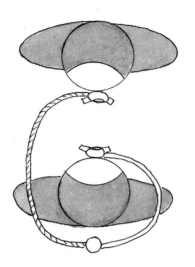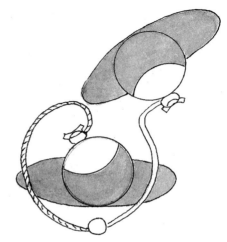

In the side-by-side and face-to-face position, if a right-handed regulator (the same as you wear over your right shoulder) is run over your left shoulder it can be offered (or taken by) the out-of-air diver in a right-side-up position with no kink in the hose. Both divers will then be breathing from right-handed regulators. If the out-of-air diver panics and takes the rescuer's primary regulator,

the rescuer can use the octopus but the hoses will be looped.

If you wear the octopus over your right shoulder it will need to be a left-handed one so that when given or taken by the out of air diver, it will be in the left-side-up position and there will be no kinks in the hose.

Look at how your and your buddy's octopuses are positioned as this may determine whether you

(Left) Left-handed octopus run over rescuer's right shoulder. (Right) Left-handed octopus run over right shoulder will have hose kink if buddy takes rescuer's primary regulator.

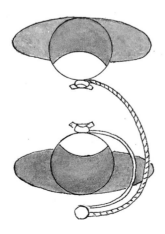

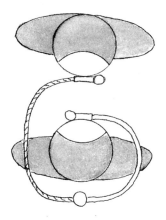

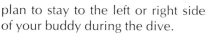

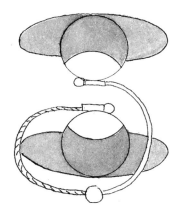

A side exhaust/ purge type of regulator can be 'rolled' to buddy in an out-of-air situation. If buddy takes rescuer's primary regulator, the roll-over style prevents hose kinking when rescuer breathes from own octopus.

plan to stay to the left or right side of your buddy during the dive.

The alternative to having to worry about right and left positioning of regulators is to opt for a regulator with side exhaust/purge buttons. The regulator can be rolled over towards the out-of-air diver or, if used by the rescuer, rolled over towards him. Some of these regulators can give a slightly 'wet' breathe, in which case it helps to tip the head and the regulator so the exhaust/purge end is slightly down, as air remains towards the top. Again, you need to plan which side of your buddy to dive on as you do not want the octopus hose pulled across your face.

To prevent kinking or 'loops' with left- or right-handed octopus regulators an extra-long octopus hose can be fitted. Another option that can be used is an omni-swivel joint, rather like a universal joint. Whether it is left or right mounted does not matter, as the swivel joint allows the regulator to move in any direction to face either the rescuer or the rescued. As an extra link between the hose and the regulator the swivel

joint can restrict air flow, so may not be suitable for deeper dives.

As with the buoyancy jacket AAS systems, if the octopus AAS system is run from one cylinder and an out-of-air situation occurs the octopus will not work!

Independent Air Supply

The main consideration when planning an AAS for wreck diving is what could happen to the divers' air supply and why. Running out of air could be due to malfunction of equipment or not monitoring air consumption properly. Wear and tear on hoses is cumulative over a period of time and a high pressure hose can blow and empty the contents of a cylinder very quickly. Damage to hoses caused by sharp edges on the wreck is another possibility. This would mean air from a sole cylinder escaping and an octopus AAS will be useless; the diver will have to use his buddy's air. The ideal solution is to carry an independent cylinder with an octopus. Thus, if the primary regulator develops a

Omni-swivel for an octopus.

A cylinder set-up with side purge regulator as the octopus.

problem, if the primary cylinder hose is damaged or in an extreme case if the diver runs out of air, he can switch to his octopus AAS cylinder. He does not have to rely completely on his buddy's air to get back to the surface.

An independent air supply is truly an alternative air source and the wreck diver should seriously consider carrying another cylinder with its own regulator, not just for emergency use by their buddy but also for themselves. A totally independent air source is highly recommended for wreck diving and is a must for wreck penetration dives.

For non-penetration wreck dives a smaller additional cylinder, with a minimum size of 3 litres called a 'pony' can be used. The pony is fixed to the main cylinder or can be hung on the front of the diver's buoyancy jacket using integrated jacket clips connected to clip mountings on the pony AAS. The regulator and contents gauge can

(Above) Pony AAS system on the main cylinder. This diver has also added an octopus to his first stage.

Front-slung Pony AAS system.

103

*Completely
independent
AAS system of
twin cylinders
with side purge
regulators on
each.*

be banded to the cylinder for neatness also to ensure quick release of the regulator if needed.

Many divers carry a pony but they have limitations because of their size, a capacity of around 3 litres. Therefore for deeper wrecks or penetration dives, twin cylinders are a practical safety consideration.

Twin cylinders should run independently of each other so one offers back-up should the other fail. This means a separate pillar valve and regulator for each cylinder.

This set of twin cylinders with manifold has an additional back-up, a pony cylinder run in the upside-down position. The diver leaves the pony turned off but if it is needed it can be easily reached and turned on.

However, using a cross-over manifold with separate cylinder valves for each cylinder means the diver does not have to remove regulators to breathe from each cylinder. This system should be further investigated by the deep wreck or wreck penetration diver, with others who have used this set-up. To keep one cylinder in readiness throughout the dive by breathing from each cylinder in turn, using one third at a time, will ensure an air supply for an AAS if needed.

105

Wearing the AAS

The diver needs to keep his hoses neat for wreck diving but AAS neatness does not mean putting it in a pocket or tucking it under other equipment to prevent damage. If needed by the buddy or the diver himself, the AAS must be released quickly. It needs to be held in place on the diver where access to it is unencumbered by other kit. It should also be highly visible, and many octopus regulators are a different or lighter colour than the primary regulator, yellow being a favourite. It is possible to buy hose protectors that wrap around or cover the hoses. As well as giving protection against scrapes, these protectors come in a range of colours, so a bright one on the AAS hose helps identify it even more clearly.

Many divers place the AAS regulator high on the front of the shoulder or centre of the chest, which offers reasonable protection from wreckage and means they or their buddy can reach it easily. In this position, should the out-of-air diver panic and take his buddy's primary regulator, the buddy can easily place his AAS in his own mouth.

For deep penetration wreck dives where moving side by side may be a problem, wearing the AAS on shoulder or chest means the diver's body will block it from the buddy. If one of the pair has a problem and has twin cylinders, he can use one as his AAS: you need to be self-suf-

ficient in narrow tunnels! Divers in this situation tend to place the octopus on a much longer hose and stow it on the cylinder with a bunjee or rubber band. If the buddy has a serious problem with his air supply, the longer hose facilitates sharing when divers are in line rather than side by side.

Wherever the alternative air system is placed, the diver's buddy must be aware of what it is, where it is, and how it releases. The buddy check is the time to 'dry-run' AAS procedures. If planning a penetration dive, the divers should practice techniques they may need to use before such dives take place. You do not want to practise using your buddy's AAS for the first time in a confined space with restricted visibility whilst inside a wreck tunnel!

In summary, the safest AAS wreck diving is completely independent twin cylinders with their own regulators. Next best would be the smaller independent cylinder, the pony, and lastly, the octopus mounted on the primary cylinder's first stage.

10 Dive Kit

This chapter looks at the kit the diver normally wears when diving but, depending upon the wreck and the extent you wish to investigate it, there are some extra considerations and items that the wreck diver needs to think about.

Suits

Sharp edges on wrecks have a magnetic attraction for dive suits! They can act like a razor blade on any suit and, as many drysuit divers will confirm, holes mean cold!

You need to maintain good buoyancy control, note where sharp edges are and keep movements to a minimum when closely investigating the wreck structure. Wild gestures to your buddy indicating the porthole you have just found tucked between jagged plates may mean a wet retrieval of your trophy!

Rust can be washed off after the dive but handling bits of wreckage covered with grease or oil may leave a permanent reminder of that dive on your suit! Some divers use overalls to protect their suits. These are cheap and can be purchased from 'working wear' shops. However, all they do is protect against the 'grime factor'; splitting and tearing with abrasion, they can offer little protection against cuts.

A 'grovelling' diver (one who likes to rummage around wrecks as though they were bran tubs at a Christmas Fayre!) must be prepared to risk the odd puncture to his suit, but extra patches on knees, elbows and the seat of the suit will help to prevent too many occurring. Some dive suit manufacturers do produce extra heavy-duty suits for this purpose but at a price.

Buoyancy Jackets

The same problems that might affect your dive suit apply to your buoyancy jacket. Whether you use your suit or a buoyancy device to control buoyancy, ensure that valve connectors and dump mechanisms are working properly. Remember, buoyancy control is critical on a wreck dive. Keep hoses neat by running them through hose retainers that are integrated in the design of most buoyancy jackets. Jackets usually have D rings or clip points where you can attach additional clip-on plastic hose retainers if necessary.

The buoyancy jacket, with all of the attaching points it offers, tends to get covered with lots of extra dive equipment so that the diver looks like a Christmas tree! Murphy's Law applies in that kit that dangles off

the jacket will get caught on wreckage. The other very important consideration is keeping the jacket's controls clear of extra kit and ensuring that deployment of an octopus is not hampered in any way.

Tidy diver (above left).

Wreck wear and tear! (above right).

Hoods

A dive hood, as well as giving thermal insulation, gives the head some protection from scrapes but not from bangs. Being aware of the surroundings and moving carefully prevent damage to the head, but for those over-enthusiastic divers who don't look where they are going, a safety helmet should be considered. Worn over the hood it protects the serious head-banging diver from severe dents!

Gloves

Hands need protection on a wreck. Even with good buoyancy there will be times when you may need to hold onto parts of the wreckage, or you use a technique called 'finger walking' – using fingers to move around the wreck without using your fins. You may want to move bits of wreckage aside to release a 'find'. Cold water dulls the skin's touch sensors and it is very easy to cut or scrape your skin underwater

Range of dive gloves.

without realizing. Back on the surface after the dive, however, you will soon know about it!

Whilst some insist on diving without gloves, they do offer the best protection. Be prepared for them to wear through very quickly if diving mainly on wrecks. Many wreck divers use fabric or leather working or gardening gloves. They are not costly so wear and tear is relatively inexpensive but they offer little or no thermal protection. To protect and give some thermal protection, there is an extensive range of diving gloves available; the ones to look out for are those that have reinforced palms and fingers, usually by a form of plastic coating.

Fins

Fins can suffer the effects of wreck diving. Even with very careful movement, the fins are usually the first piece of diving kit to make contact with a wreck. Fins will discolour as rust works its way into the scratches and cuts but this normally only affects the cosmetic appearance of the fin, not its performance. However, the diver needs to check the straps and the fin surface area from time to time for damage. Straps can be replaced and snags on the fin surface smoothed back so they don't catch every passing strand of seaweed on future dives.

Knives

Knives are a must for the wreck diver. With the possibility of loose rope, fishing lines and nets on a wreck there is always the danger of entanglement.

If one of a pair of divers becomes entangled, care should obviously

Selection of dive knives.

be taken not to get both caught. If it happens to you, stop, assess then act. It may be that you can solve the problem alone simply by increasing buoyancy slightly, thereby tautening the line and making it easier to identify the problem and cut. Your buddy should only approach cautiously to help if it is clear that self-help will not work. Some fishing lines and net, called monofilament, are almost invisible underwater. One precaution you can take is to use a torch even when the visibility is good. The filaments in the line catch the light and you can stop to assess how big an area you need to avoid.

Most divers have a knife to cut line if they do get caught but it is worth considering where to carry it.

More often than not it is the diver's legs that become entangled when fin straps catch the line. Knives worn on the leg also catch on line and releasing a leg knife in this situation might be a problem. You could wear the knife on your arm but the size of some divers' knives would make this impractical, so an additional smaller knife could be worn either on the arm or fixed to the buoyancy jacket where it is easily reached.

Dive knives do need maintenance. Many are left to rust in their scabbards, and a rusty knife will not cut. Keep them clean and sharpened for the rare occasion when you have to use them.

There are other cutting instruments that divers can carry quite

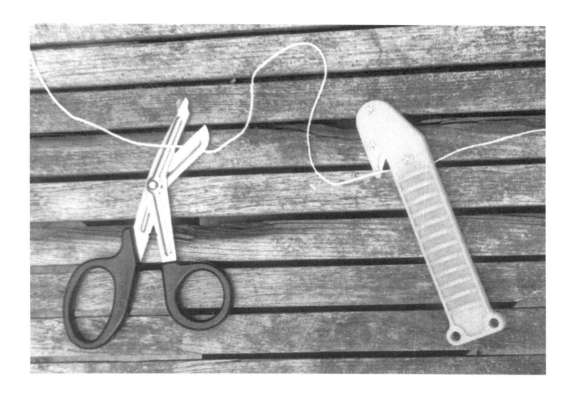

easily in a buoyancy jacket pocket. Many divers find a net cutter or small pair of 'cut through anything' shears extremely useful but, as with knives, they need to be checked regularly to ensure they are rust free and sharp.

Torches and Lamps

How well light penetrates through water depends on the water conditions. Sediment or plankton can prevent light reaching relatively shallow depths so most divers carry a torch to reveal the full spectrum of colour that lies beneath the surface that would otherwise appear to be a blue-grey hue.

A wreck has nooks and crannies where light does not penetrate and to explore it fully a diver needs a torch. Diving torches come in different sizes, shapes, types and prices. They obviously need to be completely waterproof and must be depth rated for deeper than you plan to go. They need to be robust enough to withstand the occasional knock and easy to hold and operate if gloves are being worn.

Bigger torches do not necessarily mean brighter light. The brightness depends on bulb type, the reflector design and power rating. The ideal torch gives an intense white light, but it is the reflector that governs whether it has a wide beam to light a large area or a narrow beam for localized light.

Net cutter and multi-purpose shears.

113

Larger torches, generally called lamps, are very popular as a primary light, with a reflector that gives a wide beam. What you do need to check is the burn time of the torch for the type of battery it will take. A smaller torch giving off a narrow beam of light can then be carried as a back-up light. Not only can it be used as a fall-back if the main torch should fail but it will highlight smaller items of interest on a wreck.

A dive lamp or torch is not used just so that divers can see the wreck. In dark conditions it is used by divers to signal to each other. Torch signals need to be agreed during the buddy check, along with the normal diving signals you plan to use on your dive.

Lamps and torches.

Attaching Your Torch

Wreck divers often find a dive torch or lamp that once belonged to another diver. Some of the well-dived wrecks offer a good torch (and other kit) replacement dive after a busy weekend! To keep from losing your lamp, attach it to your wrist by a lanyard or connect it to your buoyancy jacket. The back-up torch can easily be stowed in the pockets of the jacket but put a connection on this too as you may drop it when getting it out.

If you switch the torch on at the start of your dive and it becomes disconnected, you can easily relocate it by its beam. However, always remember that it may have

dropped below your planned maximum depth.

Another way of fixing a small torch so it cannot be dropped whilst leaving both hands free, is to attach it to your mask strap. Some torches are sold with their own fixing straps but plastic pull ties can be used. Torches can also be fitted to a head harness worn over a hood and a hard hat. If you want more head light, an additional torch can be added quite easily. A point worth remembering with head torches is their weight: if they are too heavy you will end up with neck strain.

Take care not to shine a torch directly at your buddy. He will be dazzled, and with the resulting loss of vision will be unable to see any signals you may be giving. Head torches need particular care just turning to check your buddy, an almost automatic action, will cause communication between you to be completely one-sided!

Other Dive Lights

There are other diving lights that can generally be termed 'locating' lights. These are either worn by the diver to mark his underwater position for his buddy in restricted visibility or attached to the wreck to mark a particular location or point of interest.

Small strobe lights can be attached to the diver's kit, usually

Two head torches, one on a strap attachment over the hood, the other fitted to the mask strap.

on the buoyancy jacket near the shoulder, so they achieve an all-round light. These are emergency lights and should only be used for that purpose. Underwater, they mark the diver should a problem arise, but some divers do use them throughout the dive. This can be very uncomfortable for their fellow diver as the constant pulsed light can cause visual disturbances. On the surface they should definitely only be used in an emergency, as they can be visible for anything up to 6 miles (10km) on a clear night. Navigation lights and emergency service lights use pulsed lights and a diver's strobe on the surface could be mistaken for one of these.

If divers want a constant light to mark their underwater position in conjunction with a torch, they can use a chemical light stick. These can also be used to mark positions on or in a wreck. Light sticks are available in both diving and camping shops. They are activated by mixing chemicals (non-toxic) inside the flexible plastic stick container. Bending the stick breaks an inner brittle vial of another chemical and shaking the stick then mixes the chemicals together. A bright glow without any heat is the result.

Light sticks come in a range of colours and sizes. A 6in (15cm) stick in yellow, orange, red or green lasts for about 12 hours. Blue or white 6in (15cm) sticks do not last as long, as the chemicals to produce them only last for about 8 hours. If you want a high-intensity light or want to light a larger area, sticks are available in larger sizes but with shorter light times.

With a small attaching point, light sticks can easily be fixed to your kit or your cylinder or alterna-

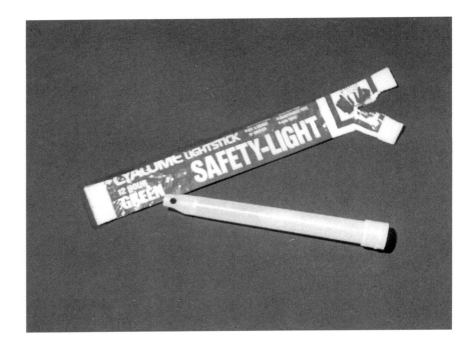

A chemical light stick.

tively tied to wreckage. With their colour range, they are ideal route markers to guide divers around or in and out of a wreck.

A night dive on a wreck can be a marvellous experience. The conditions need to be considered carefully. There should be good visibility, little or no tidal movement, experienced boat or shore cover and every diver should carry a torch with a backup. The light stick guideline to and from the shot can be used. Different marine life comes out on a wreck at night and the torch beam concentrates your focus much more than a wreck dive during the day. Because of dark surface and underwater conditions, penetration into a wreck on a night dive is potentially hazardous. If problems do arise, rescue procedures are severely hampered by the lack of light.

11 Equipment

Distance Lines

The dive plan will determine whether divers must return to the shot for their ascent. It may be required because of boat traffic in the vicinity of the dive site, surface conditions for safe pick up of divers, expected reduced visibility on the wreck or for decompression requirements. It may be a new wreck site and pilotage in reduced visibility could prove unreliable.

Selection of reels.

If the diver must maintain contact with the shot line during his dive, enabling him to return to it for his ascent, a bottom line or distance line is used. To reduce risk of entanglement, the line must be on a reel and must have a secure clip for connection to the shot.

Reels

There are many different types of reel that can be used for distance

lines. The important points to look for are that the reel should be easy to use with one hand, will hold sufficient line – generally around 50m – and is not designed in such a way that the line will become tangled around the spindle.

A ratchet-type reel, with the ratchet held open will run free; the diver simply releases the ratchet in order to lock the reel. Maintaining pressure on the ratchet can be tiring so some divers prefer to use the free-running type of reel. This will have a manual locking mechanism but once the lock is undone, the line runs freely. Relocking the mechanism requires tightening.

The size of the reel can vary. A large reel might be cumbersome and awkward to carry but easy to rewind whilst a small reel can be kept in a pocket prior to use, but reeling back to the shot need lots of effort! The reel should be slightly

(Above) Ratchet-style reel.

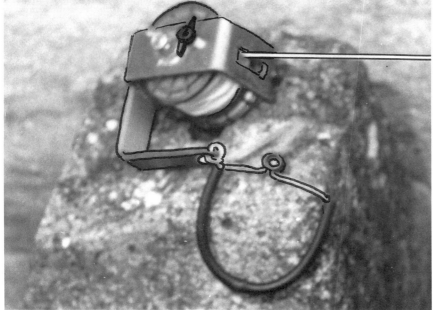

Free-running reel. The lock is the black screw on top.

119

negatively buoyant to avoid floating upwards and becoming entangled in the diver's kit during deployment. If hand-held, the reel can then be put down when the diver is stationary without it floating away.

The Line

The line on the reel ideally should not float once deployed, as it will become a hazard. Sinking line is better so that once it has been deployed and slack line has been paid out, it will rest on the wreck.

Reel with a small torch attached.

Line with a leaded core can be used but this can be quite expensive to purchase. A less costly option is to use the weighted cord which can be sewn into curtain hems, available from soft furnishing stores. Any leaded line on a reel can make it heavy to handle at the beginning and end of deployment when all the weight is on the reel. A light but sturdy reel is advisable and strong wrists are vital!

The line on the reel needs to be visible to the divers using the reel as well as to other divers on the wreck. A black or dull coloured line will merge in with the surroundings, while a white or a day-glow colour will contrast better against the background over which it is being laid and, if using a torch near or on the line, will stand out clearly. A

Looking down on divers finning away from the connection point of the distance line to the wreckage.

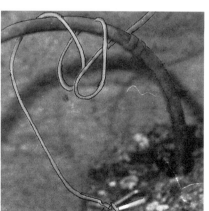

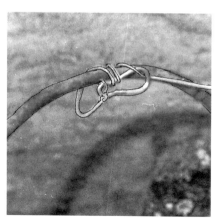

Connecting the distance line. (Left) A double turn around a secure connecting point. (Right) The karabiner is then clipped through both loops onto the line.

small torch can be secured to the reel handle and positioned so that it shines on the line, but you need to make sure it does not interfere with the reel operation.

The divers need to ensure that the line is securely attached on the shot or near to the shot on a piece of wreckage that will not cut the line. A double turn around the connecting point with a simple karabiner clipped through both loops is very secure. A karabiner with a locking system is even more secure. The diver who is handling the reel needs to ensure that as the line is reeled out it is kept reasonably taut; slack line can 'waft' and loop around wreckage or divers' fins. Remember when dive planning, to agree positions in relation to each other and the distance line. If you position yourselves either side of the line you need to ensure your fins are clear of the line. In this position, should visibility reduce, the diver not handling the reel can gently hold the line as it is reeled out and remain in buddy contact. When returning to the shot, contact may still be needed. By holding the line in front of the reel and moving slightly ahead in the side by side position, allowance is made for the diver with the reel to wind in

When crossing large gaps, belay the distance line by making a loop around an object and passing the reel through the loop. Cross the gap and repeat on the other side to prevent line sag.

smoothly without being smacked in the face by a fin!

Using the Distance Line

When using a distance line you need to remember your dive time and plan and determine how long you can reel out before needing to return to the shot. Some divers mark their lines so they know the distance from the shot.

Deploying the distance line may mean going around or over pieces of wreckage. Check that if the line is going across wreckage it is not going to be chafed or cut. If the line goes across large gaps on a wreck, take a turn in the line around something secure (belay) before crossing the gap and make another belay when you reach the other side. This prevents the line sagging into the gap as there may be divers below who could get tangled, and you would end up reeling out more line than you need.

Distance lines are not only used on a wreck to return to the shot. Pilotage back to the shot may be easy so the distance line is not needed; however, it can be useful as a marker to something of interest to the other divers in the group.

One pair of divers may find 'something' and mark it by attaching the line to it, reeling out and attaching the reel to the shot. Other divers can descend and follow the line to the point of interest. The last pair of divers in the group need to remember to disconnect the reel and return it to its owner!

When crossing open spaces, a distance line on a wreck enables easy return to the shot. When ships are broken apart on the seabed, sections quite often lie some way from the main body of the wreck and may not be easily visible. Knowing the direction in which to go to locate the separate piece of wreckage helps, but the divers may want to return to the main wreck and their shot line. By attaching the distance line to part of the main wreckage they can fin out and try to locate the other section. If they lose sight of the main wreck it is not a problem as they are connected to it by their distance line. If they find the other section they can tie off the reel, explore, and pick up the reel and return to the main wreck and their shot later.

An important point to remember is that the other piece of wreckage may stand off the seabed. Laying the distance line from the main wreck down along the seabed and up to the separate section may compromise the dive by creating a 'sawtooth' profile. It might be necessary to swim out from the main wreck but maintain depth with good buoyancy control. Line across spaces tends to droop, so reeling back to the main wreck also needs care.

Descending a shot line to a wreck in reduced visibility is not many divers' idea of fun. Where did the shot land and what in? What am I going into? Do I continue with this dive? If you do not feel happy, abort the dive. We dive for fun, not to scare ourselves stupid! If you decide to continue then fins first is the safest way – if anything hits metal or wood as you descend, better to be your fins than your head!

Distance line connected to a dropper knot for search above the shot depth.

With prior planning you should know the depth to the deck and seabed or into the holds. You should monitor your depth carefully as you descend. If you reach deck depth but nothing has come into view, stop and look around. To continue down the line may take you into a hold or down the side of the wreck to the seabed. You could use a distance line from the shot by tying a dropper knot (*see* Chapter 7) or, if possible, clipping through the shot line to make a secure connection. Just wrapping the distance line around the shot is not secure: it may sink further down.

You can then reel away from the shot staying at a level depth with good buoyancy control. If you do find wreckage you may be able to continue your dive but remember how long it took you to find to allow sufficient time for your return to the shot. You also need to monitor your depth. Moving up the wreckage and then having to redescend to the shot where the distance line is connected may compromise your dive profile.

Wreck penetration with a distance line.

Distance Lines and Penetration Dives

For extended penetration dives specialist skills, techniques and training are required (*see* Chapter 8). For limited penetration where divers are planning to enter a wreck, even if not very far, great care still needs to be taken. To fin inside a wreck 'just to have a look' can be hazardous; you may get lost and not be able to find your way out.

Dive with a buddy who likes the same type of diving as you. Arrange who is doing what, your line positions and air check signals to abide by the 'rule of thirds'. Have a torch each and a back-up light, perhaps take some light sticks in your pocket and always inform the dive marshal of your intentions.

Where penetration is restricted by exit/entry size, but beyond the entrance, the inside of the wreck appears to open up to allow you and your buddy to investigate, use a distance line. You need to tie off the distance line securely outside your entry point and, for safety, tie off again at or

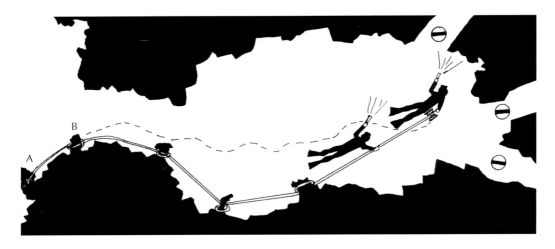

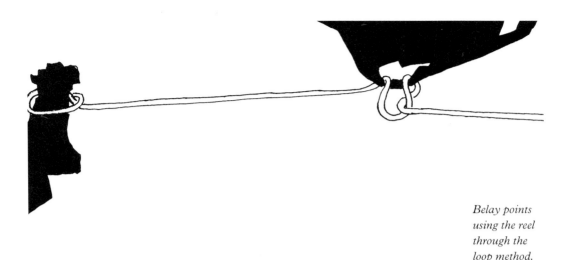

Belay points using the reel through the loop method.

just inside the entry point. By running the line out, keeping it as straight as possible and checking that it does not chafe or get cut on wreckage, you can both enter the wreck, possibly side by side or one in front of the other. Keep contact with the line either by controlling the reel or, as the buddy, gently running your hand along the line. Adopt the knees-bent, fins-up position to prevent you from snagging the line, and keep other kit secured so it does not dangle across the line. You must be prepared for the visibility to reduce – your movements and bubbles will lift silt and rust but you maintain contact with your exit point via the distance line, and this will guide you back out of the wreck.

Continually check all around you, not just straight ahead: is it safe to proceed? If not, return to the entry point. If the wreck does open up and you can explore as a buddy pair, do not be tempted to leave the line. Keep contact with it and look back to see how it lies. Floating or wafting line behind you (the dotted

line in the figure opposite) could cause a problem on your return, particularly if the visibility has been reduced. Look for possible belay points to keep the line as straight as possible to avoid entanglement on your way out.

There are various methods you can use to belay. Some divers carry belay connectors with them. A simple one is a karabiner on a piece of line that can be looped through a piece of wreckage. The karabiner is

String belay connectors.

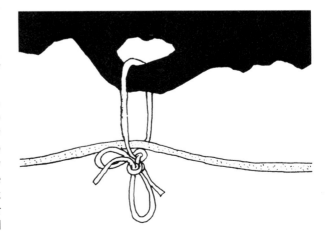

connected over the distance line. Another method is to carry string ties in your pocket. String can feed through small gaps and by tying a simple bow loop you can belay the line through it. Both the karabiner and bow methods secure the line but allow movement as you put tension on the distance line when moving ahead. They are easy to undo on your return but remember to collect the ties as any loose line left in a wreck could create a problem for other divers. For a permanent line, one that is being laid for other divers in your group to use after you, your belay points should be as secure as possible. When finished with the line, do not leave it. Lines left on wrecks degenerate and can become a dangerous hazard to other divers in the future.

If, on your penetration, you get to the point where the space you are in gets smaller or divides into smaller tunnels, do not go any further. You are now at the limit where extended penetration begins. You and your buddy should return via the distance line to your exit.

As well as monitoring the conditions, your orientation and your guide line, you must maintain a careful watch on your air. Apprehension if the visibility reduces or excitement in what you may find can increase air consumption.

As an added safety measure, another pair of divers can station themselves outside your entry/exit point. They can (nicely!) prevent other divers from entering your part of the wreck or interfering with your line until you return. Let them know your plan and how long you intend to be – being overdue at the entry point may mean you need help. If no one is prepared to 'baby-sit' the wreck for you, a slate attached to your tie-off point with a note that the line is in use ('please leave: divers on the line') is a good idea.

A normal distance line can be used for this type of penetration but it is far better is to have a dedicated 'penetration reel' with thicker line which is both able to withstand abrasion and easier to hold. A bright colour will show up more clearly in torch light. A ratchet reel is not ideal as you need to maintain tension on the spring to allow the line to reel out. Cave divers use open and enclosed reels, both of which have their own problems with deployment so it is a matter of choice. Ask for advice from experienced cave or extended penetration divers and, most importantly, practise with the reel before doing any penetration. It is far better to iron out deployment problems in an open space rather than inside a wreck with restricted visibility.

Delayed Surface Marker Buoys

Delayed Surface Marker Buoys, (DSMBs), are buoys on lines deployed underwater by divers. In effect, a DSMB is a diver's portable shot line, except that it is the diver himself that maintains tension on the line rather than a shot weight in contact with the seabed. Its use is not restricted to wreck diving. Many divers carry one as part of their normal diving kit as a safety item in case of underwater separation, or if

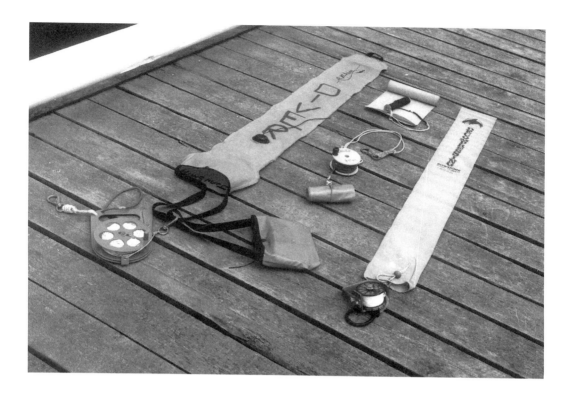

a dive has to be terminated before they are able to return to the shot.

The principle is to fill a buoy with air, which then ascends to the surface connected to the diver by a line. The buoy and line, on reaching the surface, mark the diver's underwater position and the diver ascends the line to return to the surface. The boat cover can maintain a watch and collect the diver when he surfaces.

The use of DSMBs must be planned. If the dive plan includes a return to the shot, then divers must adhere to that plan. If they think, when descending the shot, that the underwater conditions mean there might be a chance that they will not find their way back to the shot, they should deploy a distance line.

The dive plan, if not requiring return to the shot, should ensure that all divers carry a DSMB for their ascent. The dive marshal should know which DSMB belongs to whom. Colour or identification in indelible ink helps the marshal identify who is ascending from his dive, particularly when a wreck site is busy with other divers.

There are two types of DSMB. One has to be filled from the diver's own air supply and is generally a long sausage shape with an open end where it is filled. With the simple open-ended version, tension is kept on the line as divers ascend to avoid it tipping on the surface. To prevent the possibility of tipping, an inside flap creates a non-return valve which stops air escaping from

Delayed surface marker buoys (DSMBs). The one to the right and in the centre of the photo is open-ended; the one to the left is also open-ended but with an inside flap making it a little bulkier, and it also has its own carry bag.

127

the bottom of the buoy on its ascent. An over-pressure valve is fitted to allow excess air to escape as the bag expands, so it does not burst on ascent. The sausage shape rises some way clear of the water on the surface for easy sighting by the boat cover.

The other type of DSMB is a closed buoy fitted with either a small air or CO_2 cylinder that can be turned on to fill the bag for its ascent. These DSMBs also have over-pressure valves to allow excess air to escape on the buoy's ascent.

DSMB Deployment

Many divers use a reel and line to deploy the DSMB. This allows for sufficient line to be carried on the reel to make deployment possible from the seabed or wreck. Once the buoy has surfaced, the divers can reel themselves up the line, following ascent and decompression stop procedures if required, in exactly the same way as they would with a normal SMB.

When using a DSMB you are firing an air-filled rocket to the surface so deployment needs very careful consideration to ensure diver safety. Entanglement with the line or a reel that jams could lift the diver into an uncontrolled, fast ascent.

Filling the DSMB with your air supply should be by use of an octopus second stage, exhaust bubbles or gun-type valve (attachment on a low-pressure hose used to fill lift bags). Never remove your own regulator because entanglement in the DSMB line will lift your air supply away from you and then lift you without

your air supply! If the reel jams, it will lift you as it rises and if you let go to prevent a fast ascent, you will lose contact with the DSMB.

Safe deployment of DSMBs is therefore very important and the key is to 'anchor' the system for safety wherever possible.

A line attached to the handle of the reel can be utilized to secure the DSMB to a part of the wreck. This leaves your hands free to deploy the reel and, should anything go wrong, the wreck and not you will take the strain. Check that the reel is locked or the ratchet closed, that nothing can catch in the line and that the reel-winding handle has space to spin – which it will do at high speed once the DSMB is deployed. With the buoy opened up it can be filled a little so that it is floating upright and ready for the next step.

With the screw-type locking reel mechanisms, undo the lock but ensure that you keep hold of the line as the small amount of buoyancy in the buoy may start to pull the line out. With agreed signals between you and your buddy you can fill the buoy, and as soon as you do so, release the hold on the line to allow it to rise and run the line out. The DSMB reel is anchored to the wreck as the buoy ascends at speed towards the surface. When the buoy reaches the surface, the line slackens and the anchoring point can be disconnected and ascent commenced.

For the ratchet-style reels you can fill the buoy a little more so it stands upright before final deployment while the ratchet and the tie off to the wreck takes any strain. With

Deploying the DSMB by anchoring on the wreck with two round turns and a karabiner connection (as used for a distance line).

129

The DSMB in this photo has been 'anchored' by a large karabiner.

free-running reel and decompressing, remember to engage the locking mechanism or you may sink back down. Also, when back on the surface remember to lock this type of reel: if you do not and then accidentally let go, the reel's own weight may take it back down to the seabed!

Another method of DSMB line deployment is to wind the line around a small weight. The length of line is generally about 12m, and at this depth in mid-water the diver, whilst remembering to hold onto the uninflated marker buoy, allows the weight to drop and the line to unravel. The buoy is filled with air and, when the line is allowed to run through the diver's hand, rises to the surface. The divers can ascend to a decompression stop depth or all the way to the surface, tension being maintained by the divers and the weight at the bottom of the line.

However, mid-water deployment of a DSMB, whether by reel or weighted line, can be a difficult skill to master and maintain. Monitoring of buoyancy is vital to remain at a steady depth, and so is safely controlling the filling of the buoy. Mid-water there is only one anchor point, the diver! If he can let go, fine, but if not he may be pulled to the surface, incurring potential decompression problems.

Many divers who used to use this system have changed to deploying DSMBs from the seabed or wreck just prior to ascent, using the wreck as an anchor to deploy in a safe and controlled manner. But what if there is no anchor point to secure the reel to prior to deploying the DSMB?

agreed signals you fill the buoy and as soon as you do the ratchet is depressed allowing the buoy to ascend. Because the ratchet needs to be held open until the line slackens, be prepared for vibration on the reel as the line spins out and ensure clearance away from the spinning winding handle. Once the line slackens you can disconnect from the anchor point and ascend.

On the ascent the ratchet easily locks the line at any required decompression stop depths and you can hang from the reel. If using the

Midwater deployment of DSMB.

*Double-reel
DSMB
deployment.*

Double DSMB Deployment

If all divers carry a DSMB as safety equipment the buddy pair will have two DSMBs between them. Agreement needs to be made as to whose DSMB will be used. If there are no anchor points for deployment, the diver holding the reel becomes the anchor. Should the reel jam there is a danger of being pulled upwards before releasing the reel and being separated from the DSMB and the buddy. Remember that there are two reels available so both can be utilized to counter the diver 'anchor' effect. One DSMB is prepared for deployment.

The second reel's buoy is disconnected and the clip that retained it is connected securely to the handle of the first reel. The first reel with the DSMB is deployed as before but with the second reel also prepared and held in the open position. If the DSMB reel jams, the diver holding it can let go and his buddy, holding the second reel in the open position, allows the first to rise. When the line slackens, the divers can use the second to wind up the first reel, which can be unjammed or, if there is a problem with it, be left hanging while the divers ascend the line to the DSMB on the surface.

Another DSMB anchoring system: a looped line and karabiner.

133

DSMBs can also be used from the shot line as a last resort. If the divers ascend and need to decompress but the current makes it uncomfortable (poor planning!) they can deploy a DSMB whilst using the shot line as their anchorage. They need to be careful not to allow the DSMB to tangle with the shot line. Once deployed and holding onto the reel and line they can then drift off the main shot line to decompress more comfortably.

It seems pretty obvious that deploying a DSMB is best done using both divers. The pre-dive plan

Diver surfacing with DSMB.

needs to include whose DSMB is being used, who is filling, who is controlling the reel and any signals for DSMB deployment. If the divers are not familiar with each other's kit, they should look at it and see how it works before the dive. If you carry a DSMB you not only need to practise in shallow water before deploying it from depth, but you will need to work out how you are going to organize the deployment with another diver. Signals will be need to be clear and should always be included in the buddy check when planning to use this piece of kit.

Reels

The reel being used for the distance line and the DSMB can be the same.

One dive may be using the reel and line to return to the shot. Another dive may have been planned to ascend away from the shot using the same reel with a DSMB. When a distance line may be necessary from the shot and a problem arises necessitating an ascent before returning to the shot, your reel cannot be used it is tied off to the shot. However, by dedicating one reel as a distance line and another as a complete DSMB system, you will always have access to it as a piece of safety equipment.

Carrying reels clipped to the diver can present problems, as ratchets may get knocked and line begin to run out. Buoyancy jacket pockets, if they are large enough, are ideal for carrying DSMB reels. As a safety item they should be

Neatly stowed free-running reel and DSMB.

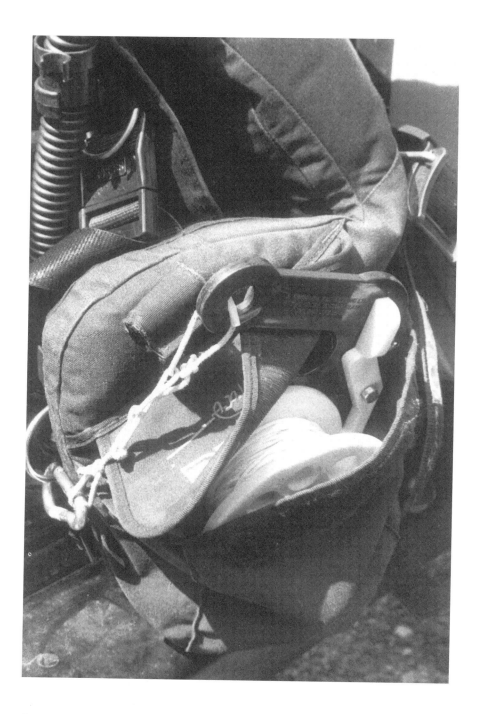

Stowing a DSMB in a large pocket. The pocket flap closes over the reel, leaving the handle outside but secured to the jacket with a karabiner.

ready for deployment with the buoy already connected to the reel. If pocket sizes are too small then stow the DSMB reel by clipping it to a securing point on the jacket. A rubber band or bungee strap around the winding handle and buoy will prevent accidental run-out and is easy to remove when the DSMB is needed. Check that free-running reels are locked securely if they are to be clipped on the jacket.

Reels need maintenance – wash them down in fresh water after every dive and check that all the mechanisms are clean and free from sand or salt deposit. The line may need to be re-reeled; if you do not check it is wound on tightly it could loop out and snag the next time you use it.

Personal Dive Flags

Dive flags are additional pieces of equipment divers can carry to show their position on the surface. Designed to be carried in their collapsed state, they are easily deployed by unfolding them; a bungee inside pulls the plastic tubes together to form a straight pole, rather like self-erecting tent poles. The flag can be strapped to the cylinder by large rubber bands (sliced car inner tubes do a good job) or it can be held in place with a sleeve on a buoyancy jacket. A karabiner connected to a ring on the jacket stops the flag from sliding through the sleeve by taking the downward strain. When needed you can unclip the karabiner and hold on

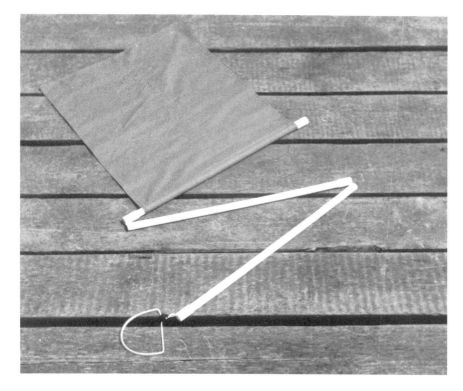

The flag unfolds.

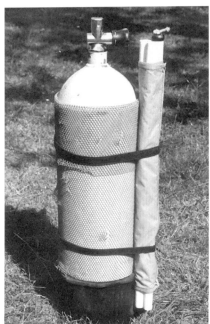

The flag erect.

*(Right)
The flag held
on the cylinder
by rubber
bands.*

*(Below)
The flag run
through the
jacket sleeve
and held by a
karabiner.*

to it as the flag slips through the sleeve and is ready for deployment.

The flag is a good back-up when diving wrecks further offshore and when surface conditions such as a large swell may make sighting of divers more difficult. In these circumstances return to the shot is normal practice but if an emergency ascent using a DSMB happens, sighting from the boat may be difficult. The flag can be used and, being usually bright red or orange and capable of rising higher than the DSMB, can be seen for quite some distance.

If a pair of divers surface they may drift further away from the boat than normal if the boat cover is dealing with other divers on the surface. A dive flag allows the boat to know where the drifting divers are and recover them later.

12 Wreck Research

Researching wrecks can be one of the most rewarding yet frustrating activities known to the diver. It requires patience, diligence, determination and, most of all, time. What you are able to find out about a wreck is directly proportional to your ability to harness all of these qualities and apply them to your task.

The reasons why divers decide to embark upon wreck research vary widely, from a serious archaeological interest to simple curiosity, and the extent to which they carry through their enquiries depends on the purpose they have in mind and the detail they require. Is this a lifetime quest to produce the 'Comprehensive Divers Guide to the Coast of Scotland,' or are we just trying to make our weekend diving expeditions a little more interesting?

Archaeological wreck research is a highly specialized subject with which I do not propose to deal to any extent in this chapter. If this is an area of particular interest to you, you should contact the appropriate marine archaeological authority.

Where Do You Start?

There are many sources of information available, but which you can use depends upon the facts you have to begin with. In a perfect world you will have the name of the vessel and the date of the loss, which makes the task reasonably straightforward. If the ship is British Registered and sank in British waters, even better, but it is not always a perfect world. However, you should remember that the British Merchant Fleet was at one point the largest in the world, and the records available in Britain do cover a large proportion of the twisted metal on the seabeds of the world.

I have divided the process of wreck research into two distinct categories: preliminary and detailed. The main difference between the two is that preliminary research can mostly be done in or near the prospective dive site, or in the comfort of your own home, having bought or borrowed a couple of easily obtainable books. Detailed research is likely to involve travelling to major libraries and spending many happy hours of painstaking page scanning or eye-dazzling microfiche perusal, if you want to avoid the expense of getting somebody to do it for you.

Many libraries provide a 'search service'; some do not charge a fee, but many do. You should, however, be aware that they will only look for what you have asked them to find. It is a job for librarians, who are unlikely to have the same passion for diving that you have and who may not feel that they have your authority to look under *Royal Viceroy*, when their brief is *Viceroy*, or check on '24 December 1937', when you said '1936'. There is no substitute for doing it yourself and my experience is that librarians are very helpful when assisting serious researchers.

Preliminary Research

Do not embark upon expensive and time-consuming research before checking carefully that 'your' wreck has not already been well documented.

There are a large number of comprehensive and easily obtainable guidebooks for divers. These are available from most dive shops, dive shows, larger bookshops, or by mail order through diving magazines. They will summarize what is currently known about diveable wrecks in a particular area. If a wreck has been located, these guides will normally give the name (if known), the position (transits and lat./long.), the depth, the best time to dive and a brief description of the wreck and its history.

Dive shops and local dive clubs are often a very good source of information about all local dive sites, including some which may not be documented anywhere else. You may, however, not wish to alert the local diving community to your new 'information', in which case you will not want to test this source. If this happens, you run the risk of duplicating work that may have already been done by others.

Local fishermen and dive boat skippers may not be divers, but the chances are that they know more about what is on the seabed in their area than you will find out in a lifetime. Information from this source might be invaluable, but you may have the same reservations about giving away information as with the local diving community.

Very little has happened at sea, particularly in coastal waters, without somebody writing about it. The local library and second-hand bookshops may reveal something that will help you fill in some gaps. Look for local books on shipwrecks, disasters, history of the port, trade, fishing industry, Coastguard history, shipbuilding, pirates, smuggling, lightkeepers' tales and so on. In addition to these unspecific reference books, you should seek out a copy of the relevant volume of the Shipwreck Index of the British Isles, the first volume of which was published in 1995 (hopefully this will be available from your own local library). All 'known' wrecks since the 1300s are listed, by area, in chronological order and the information is fairly comprehensive. If your wreck is not listed in here, you may have made a major 'find', but you will probably also have quite a search ahead of you.

Detailed Research

This is what you have to undertake if you do not find what you are looking for or, perhaps, if you wish to find out more about a wreck that has already been identified. This can be a fascinating pastime and I wish you many happy and successful hours of infuriating fun.

The way in which you should approach detailed research depends upon the facts, or possible facts, with which you start the project. Whatever the type of ship you are trying to identify, most successful research begins with the name of the vessel or the date of loss. If you have both, the task is fairly straightforward: if you have only one, it is normally not too difficult, but if you have neither, you have quite a long and tedious slog ahead of you. It is still possible to acquire information if you know who built the ship or its engines, or if you know the name of the Master (captain). You may even be able to trace a ship if you know which port it sailed from and where it was bound.

For those wishing to conduct wreck research in the United Kingdom, the largest collection of Maritime Historical and Marine Insurance documents is held at the Guildhall Library in the City of London and it is here that most research is likely to begin. This fantastic collection includes almost all of the archive records of 'Lloyd's of London' including the Loss Books, Confidential Index, Lloyd's Register of Shipping, War Loss Books, Lloyd's List and many of the Board of Trade Casualty Returns and Parliamentary Papers. This is by no means a complete list, but one can be obtained from the Library, who have produced an excellent guide to the collection. It is almost inevitable that you will end up here at some stage during your quest for information.

For the purposes of this guide I have broken down the collection into four distinct groups, based on the type of information available to you at each stage of your research.

Details of the vessels
Listing of the loss
Miscellaneous references
Reports on the loss

I have also drawn a research flow chart to guide you through the maze of sources available. This is not an infallible system, but I trust that it helps.

Details of the Vessels

The registers to look under are:

Lloyd's Register of Shipping (1764 to date minus 2 years)
Mercantile Navy List (1857–1940 and 1947–76)
Lloyd's Register of Yachts (1919–80)
Lloyd's Register of American Yachts (1927–77)

If you have a name and a date, your first record source is likely to be Lloyd's Register of Shipping. These annual, alphabetically listed records are almost complete from 1764. The register shows, among other items, name, type, tonnage, dimensions (from 1874), engines (if any), builder, date, place, owner, Master (captain), registered port and the register classification (this is the origin of the expression 'A1 at Lloyd's'). In some cases, the last year of entry will be amended to show the actual date of loss.

Research flow chart.

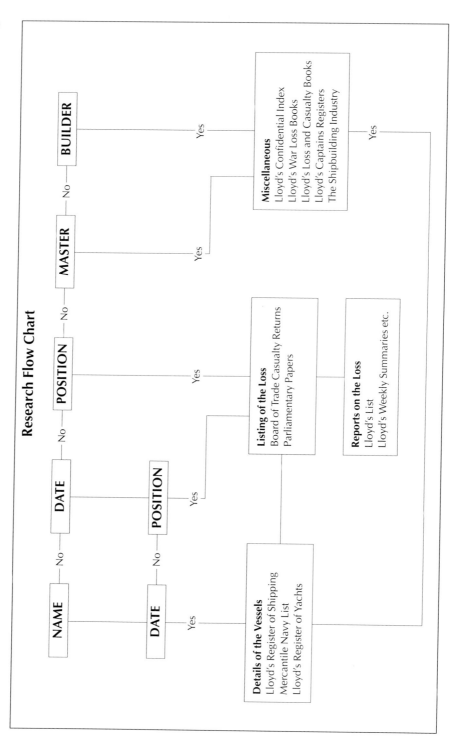

Research Flow Chart

NAME — No — DATE — No — POSITION — No — MASTER — No — BUILDER

DATE — No — POSITION

Details of the Vessels
Lloyd's Register of Shipping
Mercantile Navy List
Lloyd's Register of Yachts

Listing of the Loss
Board of Trade Casualty Returns
Parliamentary Papers

Reports on the Loss
Lloyd's List
Lloyd's Weekly Summaries etc.

Miscellaneous
Lloyd's Confidential Index
Lloyd's War Loss Books
Lloyd's Loss and Casualty Books
Lloyd's Captains Registers
The Shipbuilding Industry

There is also the Mercantile Navy List, produced as the official list by the Registrar General of Shipping and Seamen, available from 1857 onwards. This list includes many vessels not in Lloyd's Register but, unlike the Register, only lists British vessels. The details included are slightly different, but the result is similar.

Lloyd's Register of Yachts and the separate one for American (including Canadian) yachts has a similar format and can be used in the same way.

If you only have a name, but no date, the searching process is somewhat lengthened, but the principle is the same. You might decide to ask for volumes separated by a five-year gap and narrow the field down that way. Always bear in mind that using this method will only produce a possible match until you acquire other information to confirm your findings: as you will soon discover, there were several thousand registered vessels in the eighteenth and nineteenth centuries and some of them had the same name. A ship called *Jennie* is going to be harder to find than one named *Wacousta*!

Listing of the Loss

Here the relevant records are:

Board of Trade Casualty Returns (1879–1918)
Parliamentary Papers (1850–1918)
Lloyd's Register Casualty Returns (1890–1980)
Lloyd's Loss and Casualty Books

Although there are other sources, the Board of Trade Casualty Returns contained within the Parliamentary Papers from 1850–78 and bound separately from 1879–1918 are probably primarily the best source of information about a loss at sea. These list all casualties in British waters or to British ships, by date of loss. Some of the information will confirm the details you may already have gleaned from the Register, but important additional data includes the approximate (or sometimes precise) position of the wreck and a note of the voyage, cargo and number of crew (including fatalities). It is from the first of these that the date-but-no-name researchers can hopefully identify their wrecks, by referring to the position column of the list: you can then go to the vessel references to fill in the details of the vessel itself. It is also from these records that you may learn about the existence of a Board of Trade Inquiry Report, which might give a very detailed account of the incident.

If you know where and approximately when your wreck took place, this source might be your only chance of identity. You would, however, need to scour through many years of these records, looking in the position column, to find what you want. This method sometimes throws up a number of other interesting bits of information about other dive sites you may use.

The Lloyd's Register Casualty Returns overlaps with the Board of Trade Casualty Returns for a period of about twenty-eight years, but fulfills much the same purpose. After 1918 the Lloyd's Register version was the only source available. If, however, your vessel was not listed in Lloyd's Register itself, you may not be able to find it in these records, as this Casualty Register was designed to record the removal of vessels from the Register of Shipping.

The other major source in this group is the Lloyd's Loss and Casualty Books, which are kept in the manuscript section. These magnificent volumes were kept at Lloyd's to record shipping losses throughout the whole world as they were advised. As more information became known, further reports were added, so a single loss might have several entries. Without a name and at least an approximate date of loss, you may find this source to be of little use.

Miscellaneous References

Sources here are:

*Lloyd's Captains Register
*Lloyd's Confidential Index
Lloyd's War Losses: First World War
Lloyd's War Losses: Second World War
The Shipbuilding Industry: A Guide to Historical Records, by L. A. Richie

(* Exclusive to the Guildhall Lloyd's Collection)

Under this section I have included a number of books available at the Guildhall Library, some of which may also be found in your local library. In certain cases these records may be your first port of call if you do not have a name or a date for your wreck.

Lloyd's Confidential Index records the managing history of shipping companies and the vessels they operated, while all of the other titles are self-explanatory.

Reports on the Loss

The following sources may prove useful:

Lloyd's List (1741 to date, less 3 months)
Lloyd's Weekly Shipping Index (1880–1914)
Lloyd's List Weekly Summary (1880–1920)
Lloyd's Weekly Index (1914–17)
Lloyd's Daily Index (1918–27)
Lloyd's Weekly Casualty Reports (1920–85)

Lloyd's List is one of the oldest established newspapers in the world. Its purpose is to inform the underwriters at Lloyd's of shipping news, shipping movements and casualties. It was founded sometime prior to 1740, originally as a weekly, later twice weekly and, after 1837, a daily paper. The Guildhall Library Collection is complete (less 3 months) from 1741 to date. The format has changed slightly over the years, but Lloyd's List remains the researcher's bible. Lloyd's List is not confined to British vessels and many ships not included in Lloyd's Register or the Mercantile Navy List are reported on. The various summary reports are mostly weekly compilations of what appeared daily in Lloyd's List.

This might be the last hope for those who have not managed to track down their vessels in any of the previously mentioned publications, but I should warn you that two or three weeks of going through a combination of facsimile reprints, microfiche reels and actual copies of Lloyd's List could be harmful to your desire to ever dive again.

Lloyd's List will not only provide you with the details of voyages of your vessel, leading up to the date of the wreck, but will also give reports of the loss as it happened. You may also find that there are references to other organizations, who may have further details in their files, such as *The Times*, the *Daily Chronicle*, other newspapers, Reuters, the Salvage Association and the Lloyd's Agents, who will have been the first to report the majority of casualties. Access to certain of these organizations and their archives may be restricted; for example the Salvage Association may only be approached through a recognized Diving Club or Association, while Lloyd's Agents should be contacted through Lloyd's Agency Department in London.

War Losses

Merchant Vessels

War losses fall into a special category.

Research into the vessel itself should be conducted in the same way as for other merchant vessels, with the use of Lloyd's Register of Shipping and the Mercantile Navy List.

Lloyd's War Losses: First World War lists British, allied and neutral casualties. The main listing is in date order, covering vessels sunk by submarines, mines and enemy warships or aircraft. The details given include the ship's name, nationality, tonnage, cause of loss, position or approximate position and her cargo.

Lloyd's War Losses: the Second World War is set out in three volumes. Vol. 1 provides similar information to the First World War book. Vol. 2 will be of less interest to us, except for the section covering allied vessels lost to mines since the cessation of hostilities. Vol. 3 goes further and gives an alphabetical list of German, Italian and other axis power vessels lost in the war. The final part of this, covering Japanese ships, may only be of interest to those of you with expensive dreams.

Although there are many other volumes covering this subject in the Guildhall Library Collection, these two are likely to be your main source of information at this stage of your research. Both of these books are available for sale to the public, although they are very expensive. If you have an extensive library in your home town or city, it is possible that these may be available without having to travel long distances.

Lloyd's List and the various summary publications can also be used to pursue your research into war losses.

Royal Naval Ships

The information available in Public Libraries about any Royal Naval casualties is fairly limited. A few volumes of Lloyd's Register of Shipping (1779–83 and 1890–1849) and the Mercantile Navy List (1857–64, 1869 and 1871) contain lists of Royal Naval vessels and, until the middle of the nineteenth century, Lloyd's List sometimes published brief reports of naval engagements and of the movements of Royal Naval vessels.

You may find a number of books (*Jane's Fighting Ships* and *Ships of the Royal Navy*) at the Guildhall or in your local library, but details of the ship's loss and the position of their final resting place are scarce.

How Do I Use this Information?

Having described the possible methods of research and the sources of information available to us as divers, I list a few scenarios that an ordinary diver might encounter and then go through the steps we might take to investigate the wreck.

1. You have heard a story about a ship that sank in the bay just along the coast at the end of the nineteenth century, and your source thinks it was called the *Viceroy*. The story goes that it was carrying copper wire and timber, was caught in a huge storm and foundered with the loss of all hands. What a fantastic project for the club to locate and dive it.

2. You were having a gentle drift dive, looking for a few scallops for dinner, when you came across a large piece of wreckage that you weren't expecting. Fortunately you were able to mark the spot, took some transits and returned the following weekend to have a better look. You discover that it is only a part of a wreck, boilers, engine room and so on, and there are no identifying signs except for a brass plate off one of the engines, displaying the name of the manufacturer and a date. How can you discover what you have found?

3. Your favourite hard-boat skipper tells you that he caught one of his lobster pots on a lump of something about five miles offshore. He very kindly offers to take you out to dive it, on the condition that you look for and recover his pot. He puts you straight onto an immaculate, rather small, submarine, but there do not appear to be any markings on it. How can you find out more about it?

4. You have dived the *John Edwin Longstaff* a couple of dozen times in the close company of half of the rest of the diving community of the south of England. Now you have heard that there was another ship that was torpedoed and sunk in the attack on the same convoy that night and it must have gone down in the same area. Why has nobody ever found it?

5. You are having a few beers on a Saturday night in the local hostelry after your day's diving has just been washed out. You get chatting to an old sea dog in the

corner and, after you have just poured next week's wages into his hollow legs, he starts to talk about his nightmare experience before the war. He has never told anybody about this before, because the memory is too terrible, but another pint of scrumpy with a rum chaser will help him sleep if he retells his story.

'It was Christmas Eve in 1936: I was the Second Mate on the *Island Maid*, a sturdy little ore carrier of 1,500 tons and we were making for Glasgow after a long crossing from Central America, with a very special and secret cargo – I don't remember anything else and it was Good Friday of 1937 before I woke up in a Hospital in Oban. I think I was the only survivor.'

The landlord threw you out at two in the morning and your companion for the evening walked home as if he had just left the vicar's tea party. Over your aspirin breakfast the next morning, you wonder if there could be any truth in the tale from last night. Can you check it out?

Having outlined the extent of the research material which is available to us, let us look at these scenarios. Is it sensible for us to enter into a research programme, with any real prospect of success?

Scenario 1

We have a name (*Viceroy*), an approximate date (1875 to 1900) and we know where she went down (South Devon Coast).

Check your facts as much as possible: is your source sure about the name? Can he be more precise about the date? Once you have gleaned as much as you can, you should first get hold of a copy of the local diver guide books and the relevant volume of Shipwreck Index of the British Isles. If these draw a blank, then it's down to the local library and a trawl round the second-hand bookshops.

The Shipwreck Index appears to be fairly comprehensive, but have they missed one? If you can get up to the Guildhall Library, you shouldn't have to refer to more than twenty volumes, which you should be able to do in a day. You will kick yourself if you don't and somebody turns it up in a couple of years' time, so it might be worth a shot.

Scenario 2

We have no name but we do have a date when she was built, and we do know exactly where she went down. We also know the name of the engine builder.

Before resorting to libraries, it would probably be worth conducting a search to see if the bow section is close by: it is not unusual for a ship to have broken up on the surface and each section sink some distance apart. You should also check the local diver guide books and the Shipwreck Index, to be sure that the wreck, or the other half of it, has not already been identified.

There are two ways in which you could approach this research: there is a book called *The Shipbuilding Industry: A guide to Historical*

Records edited by L. A. Richie, which might give a lead to the engine manufacturer, who should still be able to identify the ship for which the engines were built. Lloyd's Register of Shipping also lists shipbuilders from 1890 onwards. It is possible that the first may be available from your local library, but both are held at the Guildhall Library. If you can get a name for your vessel, the research becomes a relatively straightforward task.

Alternatively, you might have a long slog through the Board of Trade Casualty Returns ahead of you, beginning at the date of manufacture and keeping your eye on the position column in the lists. It is possible that this will bear fruit, but be prepared for a long struggle and possible disappointment.

Scenario 3

We have no name and no date, but we do know exactly where she went down. We also know what type of vessel she is. This is obviously a Royal Navy or foreign naval vessel.

It is highly unlikely that the Admiralty do not know about the existence and position of this wreck. It is also fairly certain that she is a War Grave, so all the rules about War Graves, described in Chapter 1, should be followed. If the Admiralty do not know about it, they would surely be very pleased to be told and they should be told.

My suggestion would be that you contact the Receiver of Wreck, who will then inform the Admiralty and let you know, in due course, of the outcome of that contact. Whatever the circumstances, treat the wreck with respect.

Scenario 4

We have no name and no date, but we should quickly be able to find the date. We also think we know the area where she went down.

This may prove to be a hopeless case, but there is a faint chance. You can find your date from the well-documented details of the *John Edwin Longstaff* from any local dive guide. Being a war loss, there are a couple of sources to be consulted before you put the report down to unfounded rumour. The dive guide books and the Shipwreck Index should be your first choice and, given the fact that is was a convoy loss, therefore likely to be well documented, Lloyd's War Losses: the Second World War; if it doesn't appear there you really should concede defeat.

Scenario 5

Whilst this might seem like the wildest of tales, you will in fact find that it is the easiest to research, because you have a name and a date. A couple of hours at the library should confirm the story or expose it as fiction. It may be that the sea dog has told the story to 100 other divers before you, but perhaps they have all dismissed it as a load of old nonsense.

By the time that you have conducted your research this far and spent a few days or weeks at the Guildhall

Library, you will have become aware of the enormous expanse of information that can be gleaned from the vast array of books, manuscripts and other documents, both there and at other libraries or depositories. Either your taste buds will have been irrevocably whetted or you may never wish to set eyes upon another copy of Lloyd's List ever again.

Happy hunting!

13 Future Technology

Will wreck diving be different in the future?

Diving equipment technology is ever changing. One piece of equipment being introduced into the recreational diving market is the Rebreather. The Rebreather allows the diver to carry a smaller amount of air than in a normal diving cylinder because, by use of a filter system, it recycles air that would have otherwise been exhausted into the surrounding water. At the present time they are quite expensive and have associated servicing and maintenance costs, but their future potential is enormous.

The gas mixes that are used for recreational diving are also changing. In the past, recreational divers have just dived on compressed air but now Nitrox, a gas mix with a higher level of oxygen than normal air, is used by divers who have completed the prerequisite training courses. On a simple level, Nitrox offers longer dive times at shallow depths, but it does not increase deep diving time. It can be used on more advanced dives as a decompression gas. Reducing the nitrogen content of the mix and adding more oxygen has benefits for the diver, including less risk of nitrogen narcosis and lowering risks associated with decompression illness. It is not a 'magic' gas, however; divers still have to understand the problems associated with diving a higher percentage of oxygen in their breathing mix, follow Nitrox tables or computer requirements and be trained in its use and equipment considerations.

Tri-mix diving is also another area that some recreational divers are interested in. Again, specialist training is needed.

Virtual reality may assist in helping the diver's orientation and planning of a particular wreck dive. The wreck layout and route to be followed, what equipment is needed, depth and time checks can be incorporated into a simulated dive without getting wet!

Equipment and different gas mixes will evolve and depth and time considerations will alter, but will they affect the basic principles of wreck diving discussed in this book? The answer is, 'I don't think so'. A Rebreather with a gas mix may mean longer time underwater but we will still need to find and mark a wreck to dive, explore it safely using pilotage or a distance line, use a DSMB, penetrate a wreck using safety lines and use a decompression station. The rule of thirds will still apply, only in the future it may be automatically noted by a vocal dive computer worn by the diver.

A rebreather.

The practice of basic techniques allows the diver to adapt those skills for his future wreck diving. As divers we are exploring an alien environment and whatever equipment we use now or in the future, we need to train to be safe, plan what we are doing, use appropriate equipment and always respect and be aware of the underwater environment.

151

Appendix

Another Bowline

Make a loop.

*Pull line
through the
loop to form
another loop.*

*Drop end into
the loop.*

*Hold the end
and the main
line and tug on
the end.*

Pull the knot to tighten.

Useful Addresses

British Sub-Aqua Club
Telford's Quay
Ellesmere Port
South Wirral
Cheshire L65 4FY

Guildhall Library
Aldermanbury
London EC2P 2EJ

Nautical Archaeological Society
  (NAS)
c/o 19 College Road
HM Naval Base
Portsmouth PO1 3LJ

The Receiver of Wreck
The Coastguard Agency
Spring Place
105 Commercial Road
Southampton SO15 1EG

The United Kingdom Hydrographic
Office
Admiralty Way
Taunton
Somerset TA1 2DN

Index

Index